A Beginner's Guide On

PARENTING CHILDREN WITH ADHD

Understand **ADHD**, learn strategies to empower your child to **self-regulate**, **focus better**, and **manage their emotions** to be more successful and confident.

8 Step Program to Raise Thriving Kids

VIVIAN FOSTER

https://vivianfoster.com

Copyright © 2022 Vivian Foster. All rights reserved.

The content contained within this book may not be reproduced, duplicated, or transmitted without direct written permission from the author or the publisher.

Under no circumstances will any blame or legal responsibility be held against the publisher, or author, for any damages, reparation, or monetary loss due to the information contained within this book, either directly or indirectly.

Legal Notice:

This book is copyright protected. It is only for personal use. You cannot amend, distribute, sell, use, quote, or paraphrase any part, or the content within this book, without the consent of the author or publisher.

Disclaimer Notice:

Please note the information contained within this document is for educational and entertainment purposes only. All effort has been executed to present accurate, up-to-date, reliable, and complete information. No warranties of any kind are declared or implied. Readers acknowledge that the author is not engaged in the rendering of legal, financial, medical, or professional advice. The content within this book has been derived from various sources. Please consult a licensed professional before attempting any techniques outlined in this book.

By reading this document, the reader agrees that under no circumstances is the author responsible for any losses, direct or indirect, that are incurred as a result of the use of the information contained within this document, including, but not limited to, errors, omissions, or inaccuracies.

https://vivianfoster.com

TABLE OF CONTENTS

INTRODUCTION 12

1. **EXPLORING ADHD** 19

    What is ADHD 19
    Age of diagnosis 20
    ADHD and Anger or Explosiveness 21
    Three types of ADHD 22
    Does your child have ADHD? 23
    What are the causes of ADHD 24
    What doesn't cause ADHD 25
    What if it isn't ADHD at all? 27

2. **CONDITIONS CAUSED BY OR LINKED TO ADHD** 33

    School performance and ADHD 33
    Cognitive Development and Executive Functioning 34
    Learning disabilities or disorders 35
    Phonological Decoding 35
    Reward delay 35
    Alertness in children with ADHD 36
    Language Development 36
    Social, Emotional, and Behavioral Development 37
    Concurrent Psychiatric Conditions 38
    What is your child trying to communicate? 39
    Managing ADHD at home 39

3. DIAGNOSIS AND MEDICATION — 43

- Evaluation for ADHD — 44
- Choosing the right team of professionals for your child — 45
- The cost of ADHD — 47
- How does western medicine treat ADHD — 48
- How do stimulant medication work — 49
- ADHD Myths — 51
- Alternative Medication — 53

4. WHAT TO EXPECT WHEN YOUR CHILD HAS ADHD — 55

- Preschool Children with ADHD — 55
- Behavioral Programs used with Preschool Children — 57
- When is medication considered — 58
- School-aged children with ADHD — 59
- ADHD in teens — 60
- Modifiable lifestyle factors — 62
- Situations your child may thrive in — 62
- Can children outgrow ADHD — 63

5. TIPS FOR BETTER EMOTIONAL REGULATION BEFORE STARTING WITH THE EIGHT-STEP METHOD — 65

- Embracing Imperfection — 66
- Taking others' opinions with a grain of salt — 67
- Embracing discipline and shunning punishment — 69
- Avoiding blame — 69

Looking out for the positives	70
Expecting difficult days	70
Teaching by example	70
Leaning on others	71
Focus on what your child can achieve	71
Trying out different strategies	72
Choosing a winning strategy	72
Employing positive parenting strategies	73
Starting on the 8-Step Program	76

6. STEP ONE: HONE YOUR CHILD'S MOTOR SKILLS — 77

Why work on motor function	77
Upping the fun factor	80
Improving motor skills is particularly beneficial to children with ADHD	81
Games to improve motor skills	81
Building, Planning, and Sequencing skills	84

7. STEP TWO: HELP YOUR CHILD MODULATE THEIR RESPONSE TO SENSORY STIMULATION — 77

Protecting kids from sensory overload	86
Tips for children with under-responsivity	89
Tips for sensory-seeking children	90

8. **STEP THREE: TEACH YOUR CHILD SELF-AWARENESS AND ACCOUNTABILITY** 93

   Changing behaviors you know don't serve you 93
   Honesty is a gift 94
   Doing it your way 95
   Tempering self-awareness with self-acceptance 96
   All children can struggle with self-awareness 96
   Teaching self-awareness 97
   Importance of accountability 98
   Be your child's accountability partner 99
   Practical ways to promote accountability 100

9. **STEP FOUR: TEACH YOUR CHILD METACOGNITION STRATEGY** 101

   Why is Metacognition important 101
   The link between Metacognition and academic performance 103
   What are the elements of Metacognition 104
   Strategies for enhancing Metacognition in your child ... 105
   Be patient 108

10. **STEP FIVE: HELP YOUR CHILD MAKE SENSE OF SIGHTS AND SOUNDS** 65

    Visual-Spatial skills 110
    Working memory and ADHD 111

Working memory and ADHD	111
Auditory-verbal issues	111
Stepping into your child's shoes	112
Myth busting	114
Helping your child your manage their condition	115
Playing sensory games	115

11. STEP SIX: BUILD YOUR CHILD'S SELF-ESTEEM — 117

Building self-esteem in your child	119
Games that foster self-esteem	123
Mark's story	123

12. STEP SEVEN: RECOGNIZE AND ERADICATE NEGATIVE FAMILY PATTERNS — 127

Negative statements to avoid saying to your child	129
Behaviors to avoid	130
Positive Actions to take to establish healthy family habits	131
Creating an ADHD-friendly home atmosphere	132

13. STEP EIGHT: WORK ON YOUR CHILD'S PHYSICAL HEALTH AND WELL-BEING — 135

The power of observation	135
Stick to your child's physical health calendar	136
Importance of sound nutrition	137

Indoor air pollution and ADHD	138
Improving your indoor air quality	139
Creating comfort through light and sound	139
ADHD and the use of electronics	140

14. PROMOTING CALM, HEALTHY RELATIONSHIPS WITH PEERS — 143

Allowing your child to simply "be"	143
Middle school friendships	145
Honing flexibility	147
Dealing with teasing	149

15. HELPING YOUR CHILD STAY CALM AND POSITIVE AT SCHOOL — 153

Adjusting the classroom environment	154
Individualized education programs	155
Learning strategies	155
Enhancing your child's learning process at home	158
Embracing a growth mindset	159

16. LET ADHD WORK FOR YOUR CHILD — 161

Qualities associated with ADHD	163
Jobs kids with ADHD may enjoy when they are older	165

17. PRIORITIZING SELF CARE   167

The importance of exercise   168
coping with the inevitable   169

CONCLUSION   173
REFERENCES   185

https://vivianfoster.com

A FREE GIFT FOR MY READERS!

Included with your purchase of this book is your free copy of:

"Kids and Electronics 9 practical strategies to help you manage and limit your children's screen use"

Scan the QR code below to receive your free copy:

https://vivianfoster.com

What readers say about Vivian Foster

(for her first book, "Anger Management for Parents: The ultimate guide to understand your triggers, stop losing your temper, master your emotions, and raise confident children")

"The author, Vivian Foster, provides not only strategies for parents to manage their anger but also explains the psychology of anger with such depth that anyone (not just parents) can better understand its causes and triggers."

-C.R. Hurst, Author of the Jane Digby's Diary Series

"This is a much needed book and I'm so glad the author decided to write it. She does a great job of providing insights from the child's and the parents point of you. I can't think of anything that was missed in this book and I recommend it for anyone who could use the support. It's empowering to have the knowledge and understanding about your emotions and examples of ways to change circumstances. It doesn't have to be a struggle."

-Susan Rourke

"Five out of five stars! I recommend ' Vivian Foster's Anger Management for Parents' to parents, grandparents, and caregivers everywhere!"

-Dean Vargo

INTRODUCTION

Everybody is a genius.

But if you judge a fish by its ability to climb a tree, it will live its whole life believing that it is stupid.

— **ANONYMOUS**

When I first meet parents with a child who has ADHD (or who has been recently diagnosed with it), they often nod their heads in understanding when I tell them that my first reaction to discovering my son, Neil, had ADHD, was one of pure relief. I will never forget that day in the paediatrician's office when my husband, Stephen, whispered under his breath, "I knew it!" when we finally received the diagnosis. After hearing time and time again that our son "would grow out of it," "was just energetic like everyone else his age," or "was only reacting to our anxiety about his behavior," it was like music to our ears to know that our gut instincts—that our child had ADHD—were right.

Prior to receiving Neil's diagnosis, Stephen and I sometimes felt a little like the parents in the 1845 illustration, Fidgety Philip, by German physician Dr. Heinrich Hoffman. This illustrated poem was one of the earliest to describe—in a humorous, anecdotal way— what living with ADHD is like. The poem centers on a little boy called Philip whose parents try to see "if he is able to sit still for once at a table." Little Phil has the time of his life as he wriggles, giggles, and swings his chair back and forth. In the meantime, his parents become increasingly frustrated until not a single dish, glass, or piece of cutlery is on the table, for their little boy manages to pull the entire contents of the table to the floor, along with the tablecloth.

The tale may be an exaggeration (as comedic literature generally is), but the frustration felt by parents and siblings of children who are impulsive, hyperactive, and/or inattentive can be very real. Frustration, confusion, and fear can be particularly strong when you are not aware of what ADHD is or when you have not seen this disorder up-close in your own family.

Stephen and I have a good life in Florida, where he works as a sociologist, and I work as a teacher. In addition to having an interest in educational subjects, I am also passionate about psychology, which I have been studying and reading up on for many years. In 2003, our daughter, Claire was born, and she was what other parents used to call "an ideal child." Bright, bubbly, and capable of reading or drawing for what seemed like hours on end from a very young age. Although Stephen and I both worked full-time, Stephen's parents lived one street down and we had a trustworthy group of friends, all of whom used to share babysitting duties with us and whom we enjoyed socializing with for the typical weekend walk around the park or backyard barbecue.

Claire desperately wanted a sibling, and in 2008, Neil came into this world. He was a happy, energetic baby that grew into a toddler who quickly learned to walk and would take great delight in running from one side of the house to the other. By the time he was around four, he used to rock in his chair, pull things out of his sister's hands, and get very frustrated if he had to wait his turn.

In the beginning, we thought he was just displaying typical behavior for his age, but things took a turn for the worse when he started school. There were almost daily "talks" at pick-up time from his teacher about his refusal to sit still or let others speak and his teacher was concerned when other kids didn't want to play with him. I began to see what they were talking about when, one day at the playground, I saw other children form a literal circle and tell him to stay out of it. At this time, I decided to see his pediatrician. After conducting a few tests, his pediatrician suggested he might have ADHD. Soon after, formal testing proved her right.

A couple of years after Neil's diagnosis, I already felt more confident about my knowledge of ADHD. I had been to various professionals, including child psychiatrists, nurse practitioners, and psychologists.

I decided to be an advocate for him, not just a follower of "standard" recommendations from doctors, nurses, and pamphlets on ADHD. Every child is unique and there is no cookie-cutter "fix" for ADHD. In my experience, things really started changing when I began to use an eight-step program with Neil. I tackled his disorder from various perspective: utilizing movement, sensory games, emotional interaction and thinking protocols, activities that strengthened his motor skills, and self-esteem building. I also learned how to identify and eradicate negative family patterns and create a positive physical environment for my son. Finally, I learned to prioritize self-care so I could be my best self for my son every day.

Over the years, I shared my method with other families and found that so many experienced the same positive results. Some components of the method will "click" almost immediately, while others will take plenty of practice before they achieve the desired results or clash with your child's personality and preferences. Try the methods out, jot down your results, try them again another day, and repeat all these steps various times. Patience is very much a defining virtue of parents of children with ADHD, but curiosity, commitment, tenacity, and the willingness to try new things out are also important.

While trying out my method, bear in mind that time flies. Your child, who may have made life seem like an uphill battle sometimes, will also give you the biggest laughs, immerse you in their immense creativity, and introduce you to a magical way of viewing the world.

Time goes by.

Your child grows.

They take the lessons you teach them and become a man or woman. They learn, work, start a family, and build a career. Suddenly, you miss them terribly and know that if you could, you would do it all over again.

I hope my book helps make this ride as joyful, positive, and illuminating as possible. Few people you encounter in your lifetime will teach you as much as your child will. I instinctively knew this the first time I looked into my son's eyes.

https://vivianfoster.com

EXPLORING ADHD

In this chapter, we will delve into the nature of ADHD and its causes, learn how it is diagnosed, and discover associated conditions. I will also discuss the possibility that the signs that may perplex you are actually simply your child "being a child." Children sometimes have unique ways of dealing with the issues that cause them worry or anxiety and it is important to distinguish between typical behaviors and those that may indicate the presence of ADHD.

What is ADHD?

ADHD, which stands for attention-deficit/hyperactivity disorder, is a medical condition affecting around 9.4 percent of children aged two to seventeen and 2.5 to 4.4 percent of adults in the US (Centers for Disease Control and Prevention, 2021).

People with ADHD have differences in brain development and activity that affect their ability to self-regulate, focus, and sit still. ADHD may also affect a child's ability to get on with others or succeed at school.

Because children are still growing and maturing, it is normal for them to occasionally have trouble focusing or paying attention to a task at home or at school. Usually, children outgrow these traits. In children with ADHD, however, the symptoms may continue or be severe. Typical signs and symptoms include:

- Frequent daydreaming.
- Fidgeting or squirming in their seats.
- Finding it difficult to stay seated.
- Talking a lot.
- Having trouble waiting for one's turn.
- Having difficulty making friends.
- Indulging in risk-taking behavior.
- Making careless mistakes at school.

Age of Diagnosis

The average age for an ADHD diagnosis is seven years old, though symptoms commonly appear between the ages of three and six.

ADHD and Anger or Explosiveness

ADHD can sometimes manifest itself in angry or explosive behavior because it can interfere with a child's ability to respond to angry feelings in healthy ways. Irritability, emotional dysregulation, and anger issues can all contribute to the burden ADHD can have on a child so, from the very start, it is important for parents to take a calm approach to the situation.

By being their child's role models and modeling skills like positive conflict resolution and anger management, parents can teach their children how to react appropriately when things get overwhelming. They can also work to reduce or eliminate the many sources of stress and anger that a child with ADHD can face using behavioral strategies to help them cope with school and social demands and responsibilities. We will delve into all these strategies in the chapters that follow.

I don't believe in labeling a child as "explosive," as this can affect the way a parent interacts with them and lead to negative self-perception. In this book, I will be focusing on the positive solutions and strategies which you as a parent can rely on to help your child overcome challenges and become a more well-rounded and mature individual so they can reach their true potential.

The strategies we will discuss here, if implemented diligently, will teach your child how to self-regulate, own their behaviors, and process situations and information in a productive way.

With your help and guidance, these behavioral tools can have a positive impact on the severity and frequency of any explosive or angry outbursts your child may currently have.

Three types of ADHD

There are three types of ADHD:

- **Inattentinve:**

    Children or adults with predominantly inattentive symptoms may daydream in class, find it difficult to focus on a task or complete it, or find it hard to pay attention to a conversation. They may also be easily distracted, lose things, and forget about their chores or daily tasks.

- **Hyperactive-Impulsive:**

    Children or adults with this type of ADHD may fidget, interrupt others, or take over conversations, take things from others, find it difficult to wait for their turn, not listen to directions, and have more accidents than others.

- **Combined:**

    People may also display a combination of both types of ADHD.

Does Your Child have ADHD?
Take an online quiz.

There are many online resources parents can take if they are wondering whether or not their child may have ADHD. Parents in doubt should see an experienced professional for a diagnosis, but an online test can give them greater insight on whether or not they should consider taking the next step. Brain Balance has a useful test (Brain Balance, n.d.) that asks parents to tick boxes if specific statements apply to their child.

These assertions include: "My child has difficulty staying seated at dinner," "My child argues about everything," or "My child frequently interrupts others and doesn't let them get a word in."

The American Psychiatric Association has defined criteria for diagnosing ADHD in children and adults. These are published in the Diagnostic and Statistical Manual of Mental Disorders Fifth Edition, commonly known as DSM-5. For children under the age of seventeen, a diagnosis of ADHD requires the presence of six or more symptoms of hyperactivity and impulsivity or the same number of symptoms of inattention. For teens aged seventeen and upward and adults, five or more of these symptoms are required.

What Are the Causes of ADHD?

Recent research has revealed that there can be many possible causes or risk factors for ADHD. These include:

- **Genetics and Heredity:**

    ADHD often runs in families. For instance, a child with ADHD has a 25 percent probability of having a parent with this disorder. There is also a chance that another family member (such as a brother or sister) has it. Sometimes, parents receive their own diagnosis when their child receives theirs.

- **Traumatic brain injuries**
- **Premature birth**
- **Exposure to potential toxins such as alcohol or tobacco during a mother's pregnancy.**
- **Brain anatomy and function:**

    Some parts of the brain may be a little smaller in size or take longer to mature in children with ADHD (Rawe, n.d.). These include the caudate nucleus (which is important for decision-making and carrying out actions with a purpose), the cerebral cortex (which plays a role in emotional regulation), the putamen (which aids with memory, learning, and movement regulation), the hippocampus (key in long-term and working memory functions), the amygdala (which plays important roles in emotion and behavior), and the nucleus accumbens (which is involved in motivation, mood, and pleasure).

It is important to note that studies do not support the link between intelligence and brain size. These five regions may be smaller for various reasons—for instance, they may simply be arranged differently or have different support tissue (CHADD, 2017). When it comes to the brain, bigger does not necessarily mean smarter.

What Doesn't Cause ADHD?

It is also important to identify myths associated with ADHD. Unfortunately, until recently, very little was known about ADHD, and parents were sometimes unfairly accused of having poor parenting styles, feeding their child a diet that caused the disorder, or "causing" their children's ADHD by allowing them to play video games.

ADHD cannot be attributed to factors such as stress or poverty. This doesn't mean that parents shouldn't decide to limit or reduce their child's on-screen time for other health reasons and, of course, children who miss out on sleep because they are playing on screens all day can have worse symptoms than those who are well-rested.

It is equally important to understand that children may display some symptoms associated with ADHD without having it. They may simply be restless, or their way of thinking or being may not align with the world they are expected to conform to. Moreover, although factors such as a lack of sleep do not cause ADHD, they may exacerbate symptoms, which is why establishing a routine and ensuring your child gets a good night's sleep every night is important.

A parent of one of my students once wrote me an email that showed the extent to which different strategies can work differently with each specific child. She wrote, "I found that when my daughter, Sarah, completely stopped using all electronic devices—such as her tablet, smartphone, and computer gaming systems—her symptoms improved dramatically. It was almost as if her brain was completely rewired. I think in part this is because Sarah is very energetic as it is, and these devices push her over the edge—this is the case even when she uses these devices for half an hour or less. I think it also has a bit to do with the way that kids' content is set up to capture their audience's attention.

A typical game or video snippet can have flashing lights, fast animations, and loud colors. For a child who is highly reactive to sensory stimulation, the information can be too much, and the result can range from a refusal to do certain tasks to shouting, irritability, and more. When Sarah used to use all these gadgets, I sometimes feared she might have ODD or a similar disorder but as soon as they were gone she instantly became calmer, more cooperative, and happier."

What If It Isn't ADHD At All?

Your child's health professional will have to evaluate your child's symptoms thoroughly before treatment or therapy is recommended or prescribed. Diagnosis is a complex process since there are several other reasons why your child might be having difficulties paying attention, getting on with classmates, or remaining seated during class time (Austin, n.d.). Just a few other reasons for these behaviors or symptoms are:

- **Usual age-appropriate behavior.**

    Toddlers and young children are well-known for behaviors such as running around, losing interest in activities quickly, and getting emotional and crying when someone else takes their toys or personal items. As their ability to regulate their emotions is still developing, this is to be expected and skills like learning to share may take time to master. Moreover, children mature at different ages. If you have more than one child, for instance, you may notice that one of them mastered the art of self-control at around the age of four while the other still seems to be struggling a little with this skill at age six or seven.

- **Usual age-appropriate behavior.**

    Children who are struggling to learn can sometimes manifest their frustrations through behaviors that are similar to those shown by those with ADHD.

Those who have a very high IQ, meanwhile, can also find it difficult to learn at the standard pace adopted in the average classroom.

- **Having Anxiety.**

  Children who have anxiety can sometimes find it hard to focus or to remain in one place when the "fight or flight response" kicks in. Their unwillingness to sit in one spot or be close to others during a panic attack may be confused with ADHD when, in fact, they may simply need a little space to breathe and relax.

- **Other disorders such as mood and personality disorders.**

  Children can have disorders like major depressive or bipolar disorder. Some of these conditions can be experienced concurrently with ADHD but they can also exist independently. For this reason, receiving an early diagnosis to give kids a good start at learning and social interaction is key.

- **Oppositional defiant disorder.**

  This disorder can also coexist with ADHD or stand alone. Oppositional defiant disorder (ODD) is characterized by defiance; hostility toward peers, parents, and authority figures; and a lack of cooperation (Johns Hopkins Medicine, n.d.).

- **Dissociative disorders.**

    People with this type of disorder experience disconnection and a lack of continuity between thoughts, actions, memories, identity, and surroundings.

- **Medical conditions can cause children to become inattentive or impulsive.**

    A child may have an underlying hearing or vision problem that can make it hard for them to concentrate on or complete work. Taking a preventive approach and making sure a child attends all recommended health checks are important. The American Optometric Association recommends, for instance, that children have their first comprehensive eye exam with an optometrist at just six months. Despite this fact, parents often don't learn that their child needs glasses or treatment for problems like blurry vision until a teacher points out that their child is having difficulty reading the board.

In summary, your child may show traits like impulsivity, hyperactivity, and inattentiveness. They may test your (and their) limits, resist homework and other school tasks, or find it hard to sit in a chair for very long. These behaviors can be age-appropriate, occasional, and generally controllable or they can be severe and very frequent. Your parental instincts as well as your observations and experiences with other children may lead you to suspect that these traits are a sign of ADHD. This may be the case if the symptoms interfere with your child's ability to function and get on well with others in school and social settings (Providence Health & Services, n.d.).

There is also a group of disorders that can cause very similar symptoms to someone with ADHD. This group includes conduct, impulse-control, and disruptive disorders. ODD belongs in this category, and it could result in a child point-blank refusing to do a chore or do what a teacher asks. Many children with ADHD can develop ODD but the latter can manifest itself in challenging behaviors even when it exists on its own. Older children who seem inattentive and defiant could potentially have an addiction or substance-related disorder. Younger children who struggle at school may do so because they have a problem with their eyesight or their hearing.

The myriad of possible alternatives to ADHD highlights the need to obtain a diagnosis. The sooner you and your child are aware of why they feel and behave the way they do, the easier you can start feeling more in control of the situation. You can also make it a point to learn why ADHD has been both the greatest challenge and the most valued strength of so many people. Just a few famous people that may inspire you to "think ahead" and understand the type of person your child is, include gymnast Simone Biles, swimmer Michael Phelps, singer Adam Levine, and game show host and stand-up comedian Howie Mandel.

Indeed, if you've seen Howie Mandel live, you know how quick-witted and entertaining he is. He once said (Holland, 2020), "I often do things without thinking. That's my ADHD talking." The truth is that there are many professions in which speaking your truth with fewer filters than people usually use can be a blessing.

https://vivianfoster.com

CONDITIONS CAUSED BY OR LINKED TO ADHD

In addition to knowing how to identify the signs and symptoms of ADHD, learning more about concurrent conditions and relevant behaviors will enable you to manage them as soon as possible so as to reduce the impact they may have on your child. Some areas in your child's life (such as school performance) may be related to ADHD while others (such as personality disorders) may exist independently. Identifying any issues you spot is vital so you can give your health professional as much information as possible during your first visit.

School Performance and ADHD

Compared to students without ADHD, those with this disorder tend to have persistent academic difficulties that can result in lower-than-average grades, higher drop-out rates, and a lower rate of college graduation (US Department of Education, n.d.). This is because the most prevalent symptoms of ADHD—such as inattentiveness, impulsivity, and hyperactivity—can make it difficult for students to complete tasks, work on group projects, or organize their assignments. These behaviors can be reduced if treatment and support are given to a child at the right time. Therefore, it is important to obtain a diagnosis as soon as possible if you suspect your child has ADHD.

Children who display inattentive behavior can fail to listen to the teacher's instructions. They can also disrupt class activities or make careless errors. Sometimes, they may answer questions too quickly because they find it difficult to analyze and organize the required information. At other times, they may be able to take part in an activity. This tends to be the case if the subject matter is one they enjoy.

Cognitive Development and Executive Functioning

ADHD has a marked effect on cognitive performance (Claesdotter et al., 2017). Tests on children aged seven to eighteen have shown that an ADHD diagnosis hampers performance on a variety of tasks designed to capture the different aspects of executive functioning (a set of mental skills including self-control, working memory, and flexible thinking). These tasks cover spatial working memory, problem-solving skills, impulse control, simple reaction times, and more.

Learning Disabilities or Disorders

Around 50 percent of all children with ADHD have a learning disability or related condition (Silver, 2020). They may have dyslexia or auditory processing disorder, for instance, and if so, this may be the reason why they have problems remaining seated or focused. ADHD diagnoses need to be made as quickly as possible so that a child does not develop a gap in basic skills.

Phonological Decoding

Children may have difficulties with phonological decoding (the ability to decode words or non-words by sounding them out loud). This can make reading more difficult, especially if a child also has memory, learning, and other issues. Children with this issue may benefit from tutoring or the use of mnemonics (tools that can help improve and assist the memory).

Reward Delay

Children with ADHD can find it hard to evaluate potential rewards and match their behavior in order to achieve these rewards. They can lack the ability to accurately assess the magnitude of the potential reward, the time required to achieve it, or the consequences of the action. As stated by author Russell A. Barkley (2020), ADHD could be "a disturbance in a child's ability to inhibit immediate reactions to the moment so as to use information that is held in mind to guide the child's self-control with regard to time and the future." Essentially, a child with ADHD is very much "in the now." It can be very hard for them to complete work tasks that require them to focus on the future and meet set goals or targets.

Alertness in Children with ADHD

Contrary to what many people think, people with ADHD have a low (rather than a high) alertness level. Alertness implies a sustained ability to focus on targets and ignore distractors (Schneider, 2019). Thus, children with ADHD may complete a task too quickly (or impulsively) because they find it hard to stay focused or answer all the questions in a test within the required time.

Language Development

Learning the way language is structured depends, to a great extent, on working memory, executive and attentional functions, and phonological awareness. As children learn languages, they focus on relevant linguistic information and ignore irrelevant information. They need sustained focus to associate an object with a label or word and to push irrelevant information aside so they can concentrate on retaining key information. If they cannot do so, the process of language learning becomes fragmented.

Research indicates that ADHD seems to influence the appearance of language disorders much more than vice-versa (Brites, 2020). One study (Sciberras et al., 2014) found that children with ADHD are nearly three times more likely to have language problems than those without the disorder. In the study, around 40 percent of children with ADHD were found to have language-related issues, compared to 17 percent of those in a control group.

This is the case for both receptive language skills (the ability to listen and understand information) and expressive language skills (the ability to verbally articulate one's thoughts and ideas and be understood by others).

The researchers stressed that language problems can become increasingly problematic as children get older because establishing positive social relationships depends, to a great extent, on the ability to process and utilize language well.

Social, Emotional, and Behavioral Development

Children with ADHD can have social difficulties and interpersonal relationship issues and they may be at a higher risk of rejection from their peers. This can result from their inattention, hyperactivity, and other traits they may express. Negative relationships with others can contribute to the development of mood and anxiety disorders and it can cause children to feel lonely.

Social acceptance is the result of observation. We learn how to behave by being attentive to others, observing social behaviors, practicing different strategies, and using the feedback we obtain to adapt our responses. Children with ADHD may miss the details and subtleties of social interaction, and others may reject them because of it. This, in turn, may lead to fewer opportunities for children to learn from others. These problems can continue into adolescence and adulthood, so that an adult can feel like something is missing from their relationships with others without being able to pinpoint the exact problem.

Research indicates that social skills training can help. This type of training focuses on counteracting inattention, impulsivity, and hyperactivity in practical ways. Just a few successful methods include role-playing, observation, setting individual goals, visualizing one's goals, rehearsing scenarios in one's mind, using prompts, and learning important ways to make and sustain friendships (CHADD, n.d.).

Concurrent Psychiatric Conditions

The most common psychiatric conditions that occur alongside ADHD (in adults) are depression, anxiety, bipolar disorder, personality disorders, and substance abuse disorders. In children, ADHD can coexist with oppositional defiant disorder, obsessive compulsive disorder, anxiety, depression, fine and gross motor difficulties, learning disabilities, and more (Silver, 2021). It is important for parents to be vigilant of any symptoms that could indicate one or more of these conditions so that a child can receive treatment or therapy if required.

What Is Your Child Trying to Communicate?

Sometimes your child may display a specific behavior because they are trying to communicate another emotion or state. For instance, they may be restless because they are bored or are not interested in the topic being discussed in class. When a child feels that nobody understands them, frustration can intensify and they can have a tantrum or lash out at teachers, classmates, or family members. Regardless of whether or not a child has ADHD, giving them freedom and independence, encouraging their interests, and taking the time to listen to them so they can communicate their needs is vital.

Managing ADHD at Home

If your child has been diagnosed with ADHD, their health professional will be of great help in putting a behavioral management plan into action (Raising Children Network, 2021). This type of plan covers behavioral, classroom support, and energy level and tiredness strategies, as well as key social skills your child will benefit from learning. It should cover all aspects of your child's life and detail strategies for home, school, and social situations.

Once your plan is formulated, talk about it with the adults who are important in your child's life—including therapists, caregivers, and teachers. They may have useful suggestions and they will definitely be able to share strategies that, in their experience, have worked well with your child.

Just a few strategies you might adopt with your child include setting daily routines, praising them for good behavior, providing them with clear verbal instructions, and making key changes to your environment. For instance, you can reduce clutter at home, buy storage furniture for your child's toys and learning materials, and use strategies like color coding for your child's toys so that they can find anything they need quickly.

You may find that your child is more receptive at specific times of the day, that they respond more positively when you use certain words or ask them for things in a particular way, or when they are in certain locations. By contrast, some toys and games, noise, and light may exacerbate their symptoms. Be vigilant and keep a journal, listing down all relevant situations and circumstances that can help you identify your child's triggers.

Children with ADHD can benefit from strategies such as role-playing and the visualization of specific situations. For instance, you might role-play a situation that your child faces at school—such as being teased.

Ask your child how they feel about being called names, acknowledge their feelings, come up with positive ways to respond, then re-enact the situation, with your child practicing the new, socially acceptable ways to respond. Ask them to report back to you after trying out these strategies at school. When they do, congratulate them and tell them how happy you are—even if they did not practice every piece of advice you gave them.

You can also use specific hand gestures or words that serve as "prompts" for your child to do specific things such as stop, listen, or do something. For instance, when you raise your hand, it might mean "stop" or when you point to your ear it might mean "listen."

It is important to test out all the strategies your child learns with others. Organize play dates, get to know other parents at school so you build good friendships, and reward your child when they play with others in a productive way. Also, respect your child's need to rest and have a little "me time." Children who are overtired or fatigued (and those that do not get enough sleep) can find it harder to control impulses and their hyperactive behavior can intensify. Schedule breaks between activities and find relaxing activities your child enjoys (these can include building blocks and drawing or coloring). Ensure your child has all the fuel they need to be their best by feeding them a healthy diet comprising home-cooked meals made with ingredients such as lean protein sources, fruits and vegetables, nuts, and pulses.

Finally, talk about classroom strategies with your children's teacher. Let them know that your child works better when big assignments are divided into smaller ones, or that seating your child in a place where there are fewer distractions can enhance their focus. Ask if the school can provide extra support in the form of a "buddy" who can introduce them to new friends and help them learn key social interaction skills. Schools can help by creating an individual education plan for your child.

This plan can involve modifications that will aid in learning such as giving your child personalized homework, giving your child two sets of textbooks so if they leave a book at school or at home they can still progress with their work, and providing your child with a physical "shield" that goes around their desk. They can use this shield in class when the environment is crowded or busy and when distractions abound.

DIAGNOSIS AND MEDICATION

Knowing whether or not to ask a professional for a diagnosis for your child is a tough decision. For starters, you may wonder whether or not your child's behavior is simply typical of their age.

Your instinct as a parent is much more important than you might think. If you notice that your child's behaviors are severe, numerous, or consistent, then seeing a professional to obtain a diagnosis is recommendable.

As suggested, you might start out by completing an online test that is catered to parents who think their child might have ADHD. These tests ask questions aimed at eliciting whether your child might have behaviors that indicate inattentiveness, hyperactivity, and other characteristics of ADHD.

Analyze how you feel about your child's behavior and consider if you can manage their behavioral issues by trying out a few strategies at home. If you think you need a little help, know that there are dedicated professionals who are trained in teaching parents useful strategies that can make life better for the whole family.

A good first step is to talk to your child's pediatrician. They may be familiar with ADHD or have taken supplementary courses on the subject. Your pediatrician will also be able to recommend you (if necessary) to experienced, recognized, trustworthy professionals such as psychiatrists or psychologists who specialize in ADHD. Your child's school psychologist or counselor may also be able to point you in the right direction.

Evaluation for ADHD

A child can receive an evaluation for ADHD at the age of four or above. During an evaluation, a specialist (which may be a pediatrician, psychiatrist, or child psychologist) will ask you various questions regarding symptoms such as inattention, hyperactivity, and impulsivity. Their aim is to find out whether or not these behaviors are severe or frequent enough to indicate ADHD, and through their queries they will attempt to rule out other conditions.

Typical questions will cover areas such as your child's home, school, and social life. An evaluation can involve other adults such as school staff, childcare providers, and/or mental health professionals. It may include interviews with parents and their child, discussion about your family's medical history (the professional will want to know, for instance, if anyone else in the family has ADHD), behavior rating scales as completed by teachers and parents, parental observations on their parenting style, intelligence tests and screening for learning disabilities, screenings for potential medical/physical/neurodevelopmental issues, screening for the presence of visual or hearing problems, and more (CHADD, n.d.). The professional may also request to observe your child at home or at school.

The list of tests may seem overwhelming to you. Bear in mind that the more information the professional has, the easier it will be for them to point you in the right direction. During an evaluation, the professional may find your child has a vision or other problem that requires immediate treatment. Fixing these health problems can give your child a good start at school and in social settings.

Choosing the Right Team of Professionals for Your Child

There is no hard-and-fast rule when it comes to selecting the person or team that can help you select the right treatment or therapy for your child. Each professional specializes in a different area and can suggest different therapies or treatments. The person or team that oversees your child's care may include (Understood Team, n.d.):

- **Your Child's Pediatrician:**

    In addition to evaluating your child for symptoms, the pediatrician may prescribe medication, oversee your child's response to treatment, and work alongside other professionals like clinical psychologists and nurse practitioners.

- **Pediatricians specializing in child behavior and development.**
- **Pediatric neuropsychologists.**
    They can carry out a wide array of tests and provide therapy.
- **Nurse practitioners.**
    They evaluate and diagnose ADHD, while also prescribing and monitoring medication if necessary.
- **Pediatric neurologists.**
    These doctors specialize in the brain and nervous systems and they can evaluate, diagnose, and treat children with ADHD.
- **Psychiatrists.**
    They can also evaluate and diagnose children and carry out tests for concurrent conditions. They can also prescribe medications and monitor your child's progress.
- **Clinical child psychologists.**
    These professionals can diagnose children as well as provide counseling for concurrent issues like anxiety, depression, and emotional regulation.
- **Cognitive behavior or behavior therapists.**
    These professionals can help work on behavioral strategies, improve your child's social skills, help with concurrent mental issues, and more.
- **Clinical social workers.**
    They can diagnose ADHD and provide therapy to your child

- **School psychologists.**

    They can evaluate, attend meetings to set an individual education plan for your child, help teach your child behavioral and social skills, and more.

- **Educational therapists.**

    Their main focus is on helping children in academic and organizational areas.

The Cost of ADHD

There are many expenses you may incur if your child has ADHD—ranging from medication right through to therapy. Visiting a doctor alone can cost anywhere from a few hundred to almost $3,000 dollars (sometimes more, depending on the particular specialist you choose). Medication, meanwhile, could set you back between $10 to $200 per month.

The extent to which you will be covered for these costs by your insurance policy depends on your particular plan. Additional costs can be incurred for therapy (anywhere from $200 to $2,000 a month), academic support, accidents and injuries, lost items, and more. Research indicates that on average, families of children with ADHD spend $15,036 per year (not including treatment), while families of children without ADHD spent $2,848 (Castro, 2019). When calculating costs, consider the fact that parents or siblings may also benefit from mental health treatment. Caregivers can also experience a socio-emotional burden, including strained relationships between parenting partners, stress, and having difficulty taking part in social activities.

How Does Western Medicine Treat ADHD?

Parents may wish to try out a behavior-based approach rather than start kids on medication immediately upon diagnosis—particularly if their children are young. In general, this approach may be particularly successful (Cohen, 2018) if a child is only inattentive (in other words, if they do not have impulsive and hyperactive behaviors). Recent research shows that a combined approach (involving both medication and behavioral therapy) is often the approach that is recommended by professionals (Braaten, 2016). When prescribed correctly and monitored carefully by a qualified health professional, the benefits of treatment may outweigh its disadvantages. Once again it is important to research and obtain various opinions because medication can have side effects.

Common medications used to treat ADHD in children include:

- **Stimulant medications.**

    These are the most commonly prescribed for ADHD. They help improve inattention and hyperactivity by balancing neurotransmitter levels in the brain. Medications belonging to this group include Adderall, Dexedrine, and Vyvanse, which are considered amphetamines. Another group of stimulants are methylphenidates such as Ritalin, Concerta, and Focalin.

- **Other medications.**

    These include Strattera, a non-stimulant that has antidepressant properties and does not worsen tics or Tourette's Syndrome. However, Strattera seems to be less effective at quelling hyperactivity. It is sometimes recommended when children cannot take stimulants or if the latter cause serious side effects. Strattera itself can have a few side effects— including headaches, sleepiness, tummy upset, mood swings, nausea, and dizziness. This medication is additionally known to increase suicidal thoughts in some people— particularly children and young adults with ADHD who also have depression and bipolar disorders.

How Do Stimulant Medications Work?

Stimulants are believed to increase levels of the neurotransmitter dopamine, a "feel-good" neurotransmitter that is linked to attention, pleasure motivation, and movement. For people with ADHD, it can increase their ability to concentrate while reducing hyperactivity and impulsivity. Stimulants can be short or long-acting. Those that are short-acting need to be taken two or three times a day. Long-acting stimulants, meanwhile, are usually taken just once a day.

Common side effects of stimulants include headaches, restlessness, sleep issues, tummy upsets, mood swings, dizziness, and depression. There are also a number of safety concerns surrounding medications for ADHD. Their effects on the developing brain are as yet unknown and they can trigger psychiatric problems like aggression, anxiety, and depression. They can additionally affect the appetite, keep kids awake, and cause a "rebound effect" as they start to wear off. Some children who take them can seem sedated, develop tics, or become irritable or tearful (this is considered a rare side effect). All side effects should be discussed with the professionals who are monitoring the effect of medication on your child.

Stimulants have been found to cause sudden death in people with heart conditions, so the American Heart Association recommends that all children and adults have an evaluation with a cardiologist prior to taking stimulants. These medications also have a potential for abuse and parents should ensure that their child does not share their medication with anyone.

In general, stimulants are not recommended for people with heart problems, high blood pressure, severe anxiety, a history of substance abuse, glaucoma, hyperthyroidism, and other conditions. If your child displays signs such as chest pain, shortness of breath, hallucinations, paranoia, fainting, or the like, see a doctor immediately.

When talking to an ADHD specialist, ask them questions such as what treatments they recommend, whether or not they think your child's symptoms can be managed without medication, potential side effects of prescribed medications, how long your child will be on a specific medication, and what to watch out for that may indicate you need to stop the medication.

Also, ask yourself if your child has been aided through an exclusively behavioral approach.

In some cases, self-calming and behavioral approaches can help. You should also ask yourself how helpful your child's school is. Be aware that your child's symptoms may be related to exposure to toxins or undiagnosed learning problems or medical conditions.

ADHD Myths

Be aware of the following common misconceptions about ADHD (Morin, n.d.):

Myth 1: ADHD is not a medical condition.

ADHD has been recognized as such by a host of reputable institutions—including the Centers for Disease Control and Prevention, the American Psychiatric Association, and The National Institutes of Health. These institutions consider it a hereditary disorder since 25 percent of all kids with ADHD reportedly have a parent with the same disorder.

Myth 2: People with ADHD are just lazy.

Imaging studies reveal differences in brain development in people with ADHD. Their disorder has nothing to do with their attitude.

Myth 3: People with ADHD can never concentrate or focus.

Children and adults with ADHD can actually have hyperfocus, becoming very interested in a subject that fascinates them.

Myth 4: Girls don't have ADHD.

Twice as many boys as girls have ADHD. The disorder can be overlooked or undiagnosed in girls.

Myth 5: ADHD is the result of bad parenting styles.

Children with ADHD are not impulsive, inattentive, or hyperactive because of bad parenting or a lack of discipline.

Myth 6: ADHD is a child's disorder

Although some symptoms of ADHD can lessen or disappear as they grow, most people have symptoms even when they are adults. However, they can learn ways to manage their disorders over the years.

Myth 7: ADHD is a learning disability.

ADHD is sometimes concurrent with learning disabilities but it is a separate disorder. ADHD does not, per se, affect skills like reading, mathematics, or writing.

Myth 8: All children with ADHD can't sit still.

Not all children with ADHD show symptoms of hyperactivity.

Alternative Medication

You might also consider looking into alternative approaches to ADHD—including traditional Chinese medicine. The latter seeks to restore balance to the body and mind through a combination of acupressure, acupuncture, food therapy, herbal medicine, and lifestyle changes. To achieve balance, integrative specialists say (Franklin, 2017) that ADHD needs to be approached on four levels:

Level 1: Essence.

A combination of genetics and environmental factors (food, lifestyle, and more). By improving a child's nutritional intake and environment, balance can be restored.

Level 2: The Liver.

An unhealthy liver can cause irritability, hyperactivity, and irritation. By detoxifying the body, these problems can improve.

Level 3: The Digestive System.

Having a healthy gut microbiome can help restore mental and emotional health.

Level 4: The Mind.

The brain is not designed to tolerate excessive stimulation. Integrative health professionals recommend that parents limit the amount of time children are allowed to spend on technology, balancing it out with holistic stress-busting activities such as deep breathing, outdoor exercise, and sports

Deciding on the perfect combination of treatments and therapies for your child may take time and experimentation. Approach this goal patiently and with curiosity and an open mind. Use your own judgment but also rely on the expertise of a team you trust to guide you on what is sometimes a complex path.

4

What to Expect When Your Child Has ADHD

"Accept Your Child as He or She Is"

You cannot fight against the symptoms of ADHD. As a parent of a child with ADHD, one of the most important things I learned was to let my child simply be who he was, to express the myriad of emotions and thoughts he wished to share with me. When it comes to ADHD, symptoms such as hyperactivity and impulsiveness can decrease over time but even if they don't, acceptance is vital if you and your child are to move in a positive direction. ADHD has different manifestations from age to age. In this chapter, I will delve into the behaviors you might find in your child as they enter each major age group.

Preschool Children with ADHD

ADHD is most often diagnosed in children once they are at school, but younger children can also display clear signs of the disorder.

Currently, between 2 and 6 percent of preschoolers are thought to have ADHD—which is a smaller percentage than that found in school-aged kids (11 percent). All young children are active and energetic but preschool kids with ADHD can display these qualities at a much higher or more intense level. At this age, behavioral therapy is usually the chosen method, with stimulant and other treatment-based approaches only used if therapy does not work.

Common signs of ADHD in preschool-aged children include having difficulty following directions and waiting for one's turn, not paying attention, and finding it hard to stay put in one place. Children aged four who are diagnosed with ADHD also follow a very small percentage of their parents' instructions (10 percent, compared to 75 to 80 percent of children without ADHD). Indeed, this is often what prompts parents to seek help (Miller, n.d.).

In order to make a diagnosis, health professionals usually ask parents (and one or more other adults who are in close contact with the child) various questions contained in dedicated screening questionnaires. It is important to find out how the child behaves in other settings (for instance, at preschools or in the homes of family and friends) so the professional can get a clearer picture of the frequency and severity of their symptoms. The professional may also test for other potential conditions that can mimic ADHD—including anxiety, depression, or sleep issues.

Behavioral Programs Used with Preschool Children

The first line of treatment for preschool kids is behavioral therapy such as parental training. Some of the most popular programs include The Incredible Years, Positive Parenting Program (Triple P), and Parent Management Training (PMT). These aim to improve positive parent-child interactions and to teach parents skills that will help reduce behavioral issues in children. The earlier kids start the better; obtaining a diagnosis when your child is in preschool provides you with an excellent opportunity to commence this type of therapy.

Studies have shown that parental training has positive results. One study found that mothers who utilized the Triple P program reported significant improvements in areas such as maternal depression and anxiety, mother-child relationships, stress, and child behavior (Aghebati et al., 2014). Many of these programs have a long history of success. The Triple P program, for instance, started more than thirty years ago and is the subject of almost 700 published papers and hundreds of clinical trials, studies, and evaluations (CHADD, 2017).

When is Medication Considered?

Because few studies have examined the effect of long-term use of stimulants at this age, health professionals should be cautious about prescribing them. Medication is sometimes prescribed in a select number of cases, including:

- When a child does not respond to behavioral treatment.
- When a child poses a risk of injury to themselves or others.
- When a child is asked to leave daycare or preschool.
- When the child may have had a nervous system injury (including premature birth or exposure to toxic substances)
- When a parent is on the edge of a mental breakdown because of the child's behavior.

A team from the Developmental Behavioral Pediatrics Research Network (DBPNet) reviewed the medical records of close to 500 preschool children (with a mean age of five), finding that around 35 percent of them began treatment with A2A medications. These medications, which produce fewer side effects than stimulants but can produce daytime sleepiness, were initially used to regulate blood pressure in adults. However, they received FDA approval for the treatment of ADHD in school-aged children when they were found to improve focus and attention and reduce other symptoms (McCarthy, 2021).

School-Aged Children with ADHD

Children with ADHD can display behaviors such as fidgeting in class, daydreaming, interrupting the teacher or their classmates, losing their work, and finding it hard to sit still in their seats. Obtaining a diagnosis is important because children could have a learning disorder like dyslexia and act out because they are frustrated in class. Generally, children who have ADHD display similar behaviors in various settings. The aim for parents and health professionals at this age is to ensure that the child is correctly diagnosed so as to provide them with the right therapy or treatment.

Research indicates (Pfiffner & Haack, 2014) that behavior management treatments have positive effects on child compliance, ADHD symptoms, parent-child interactions, parenting, and parenting stress. Some of the programs mentioned for preschool children are also used with school-aged children. The list of approaches used with children in this age group includes Teen Triple P (used with tweens as well as teens), the Incredible Years Parenting Program (which is designed for children aged two to twelve and which has an 80 percent success rate), and **Parent-Child Interaction Therapy** (which aims to help children feel calm and good about themselves and teaches parents the skills they need to master challenging behaviors). Another popular choice is the New Forest Parenting Program (for children aged three to eleven), which takes place in the family home during eight weekly visits.

Medication may also be prescribed for a school-aged child with ADHD. The American Academy of Pediatrics recommends parental training in behavior management for kids under the age of six and a combination of medication and behavioral training for those who are six and above (Centers for Disease Control and Prevention, n.d.). Some parents choose to try out alternative approaches—including a device called the Monarch External Trigeminal Nerve Stimulation (eTNS) System, which can be used in kids aged seven to twelve who are not on ADHD medication.

ADHD in Teens

Teens with ADHD may get distracted and have poor concentration and they may have problems with their grades. They may also make decisions impulsively or fidget or move around in their seats. As is the case with younger children, they may lose their homework, not wait their turn to speak or participate in activities, interrupt others, or complete assignments too quickly. ADHD also poses a driving risk for teens, who are two to four times more likely to have a vehicle accident than peers their age without ADHD (WebMD, 2021). However, teens who drive but take their medication can significantly lower their risk of accidents.

Teens with ADHD are more likely to abuse alcohol and drugs other than marijuana. Parents can help by discussing driving privileges and talking about the risk of drugs and alcohol with their children. Moreover, ensuring their child has the right treatment can also help lower the likelihood of substance abuse.

Teens with ADHD and Relationships

Kids with ADHD have a higher risk of being bullied. Although not all teens have problems getting on with others, others can be teased or ostracized if they are shy or impulsive. Parents can help their children by encouraging social interactions, giving them key pointers about what others might expect from them at parties and other occasions, and setting up social behavior goals for their children.

Programs for Teens

Some experts believe that behavior therapy is sufficient to treat ADHD in children. However, around 80 percent of children who are prescribed medication in their younger years continue to take them in their teens as recommended by their health team. Usually, a combination of both approaches provides positive results. Specific programs like Teen Triple T teach parents five important skills: how to use assertive discipline; set realistic expectations; care for themselves; create a positive learning environment for their kids; and build a safe, interesting environment.

Some families also try out alternative treatments such as Chinese medicine, memory training, neurofeedback, and the like, often alongside medication. They can also rely on strategies such as setting clear rules for home, school, and social settings; setting a reasonable routine for their teen children;

other activities they excel at and enjoy (activities can range from science clubs right through to art, music, and indeed any hobby that ignites a child's passion).

Modifiable Lifestyle Factors

Some lifestyle factors—including watching too much television or not enjoying good sleep quantity and quality—can exacerbate ADHD symptoms or result in neurobehavioral deficits that resemble or worsen ADHD symptoms (Cassoff et al., 2012). Researchers at the ISGlobal Barcelona Institute for Global Health studied data obtained from over 800 children taking part in the INMA Project (Childhood and the Environment). They found that spending more time on cognitively stimulating activities in childhood is linked to a lower risk of the onset of ADHD symptoms. Just a few examples of cognitively stimulating activities include games and puzzles, word games, math problems, reading—anything and everything that challenges one's brain to think.

Situations Your Child May Thrive In

You may find that your child displays positive behaviors in some situations more than others. These include those in which they can receive immediate rewards for complying with instructions and moments in which they receive individual attention. Because children with ADHD may have trouble waiting for long term rewards, they tend to appreciate those ones that don't require too much focus. They also enjoy being alone with a parent or teacher because issues such as interruption or waiting for one's turn are not as problematic as they can be in a group setting.

Can Children Outgrow ADHD?

As mentioned above, most people do not "outgrow" ADHD but they can learn important ways to manage it and achieve success in work and personal relationships. One national survey found that around 50 percent of adults with ADHD are able to hold down full-time jobs, compared to 72 percent of adults without the disorder (WebMD, 2020). Adults with ADHD can also find that behaviors such as distraction, procrastination, and inattentiveness can trigger relationship conflicts.

People with ADHD can thrive both professionally and personally with the right treatment and strategies. In personal settings, useful tips for both adults and children can include setting a time to talk, actively avoiding hyperfocus during mealtimes (by encouraging a person who is hyper focused to get up and move around until they can be more "present"), and battling forgetfulness through the use of reminder and time management apps.

At work, adults with ADHD can take several steps to stay focused and meet their daily tasks. These include keeping daily online planners or calendars, working in a quiet and uncluttered space, scheduling in time for answering text messages and emails, breaking up big goals into smaller ones and setting a time for completion of each goal, and delegating time consuming tasks to an assistant so one can concentrate on more important goals.

Adults with ADHD should also try to find a good work-life balance, eat healthily, and reward themselves for their achievements.

https://vivianfoster.com

Tips for Better Emotional Regulation before Starting with the *Eight-Step Method*

It is vital to distinguish between your child and ADHD. Your child's disorder does not define them. Instead, it is something you can conquer alongside your child and you can achieve the very best results possible if you work together as a team.

When facing a disorder such as ADHD, you ultimately have two choices: you can blame others, get angry at the world, label your child as "impossible," and delegate difficult decisions to your partner. On the other hand, you can embrace positive parenting strategies (Carpenter, 2021).

Before starting on the eight-step program, I would love to share a few tips that can help you be a more accepting, proactive, and loving parent who always keeps their eye on their ultimate goal—to raise a happy, healthy child who accepts themselves as they are, is willing to work on positive change and leverages their strengths so they can shine professionally, socially, and above all, personally.

Embracing Imperfection

No child or parent is perfect. We all make mistakes, have personality traits we need to work on, and occasionally behave in a less-than-ideal manner. Some aspects of ADHD can make it difficult to live with. As parents, we have day-to-day stressors that can make it harder to exercise patience with our children when they demonstrate behaviors such as inattentiveness, a refusal to do chores, or interrupting other family members when they are speaking. Allow yourself and your child a few "bad days" but in general, try to be the kind of person your children view as positive, proactive, and confident. Children can be very sensitive and can pick up on signs that indicate that they are a "disappointment" to you.

When you have had a hard day, it can be difficult to detach yourself from stress, pain, or anger and put yourself into your child's shoes, but it is important to try. You may have had to put up with negative words from your boss, lost a client, or seen a coveted promotion go to someone else. However, think about how your child's day may have been. They might have wanted to play with children who told them to "go away." Their teacher may have reprimanded them when they got up from their seat one too many times, or they may have felt left out when they were unable to complete a task their peers easily solved.

Building confidence in a child begins with acceptance and continues with an appreciation for your child's unique traits, gifts, talents, sense of humor— indeed, everything that makes them the one-of-kind human being that they are. Children with ADHD have many amazing traits that can make life entertaining, fun, humorous, challenging, exhausting, and amazing. They can be creative, have enviable amounts of energy, and possess wonderful interpersonal skills that make them an indispensable part of your home and your heart.

Your child is destined for something great because many of the same qualities that people sometimes see as "flaws" in a child with ADHD—fast decision making, creativity, tireless enthusiasm, hyperfocus—are possessed by many great leaders, thinkers, inventors, and creatives.

Taking Others' Opinions with a Grain of Salt

If your child with ADHD is your first child, you may be shocked by the "cruel place" that playgrounds and school grounds can be. If you are an empath and you think before you speak and consider the effect your words can have on others' self-esteem, it can be very difficult to see how other parents or adults can judge your child, openly telling you or other parents that your child is "slow," "difficult," or "nervous." There are two important things to take note of when you hear a comment of this nature. The first is that the same people usually level the same type of criticism at children without ADHD as well. They feel free to point out traits in others' children yet may not be quite as open to criticism about their own.

Meeting other parents and forming a kind-of second "family" is important. Doing so will ensure you always have someone to talk to at a ball game, share carpooling duties with, and let off steam with from time to time. Choose your friends wisely, especially on school grounds. Surround yourself with those who love and support you and your child, who see the same quirky, funny, brilliant aspects of your child's personality that you and your family do. Words and judgment can, indeed, have a negative effect on your happiness and well-being.

The second tip to keep in mind when others label your child, is that every person changes immensely as they grow and mature. Try to recall what you were like as a child. I remember I was on the naughty side, talking in class, preferring the social rather than the academic side of elementary school, and always enjoying a giggle. However, by the time I was in high school, I was a much different person. Something inside me told me when it was time to buckle down and do the work I had to in order to attend my college of choice. Labeling is always to be avoided because it imprisons them inside a word, a thought, or a belief. Your child is a changeable human being that can grow, learn, and thrive. When someone tries to tell you otherwise, don't waste your energy trying to convince them that they are wrong. Be secure in the parent you are and in the child that you have.

Embracing Discipline and Shunning Punishment

Discipline is the positive, beneficial side of feedback while punishment is its negative, futile side. The problem with punishment is that it is usually no more than "the last straw" at the end of a long day. Before taking away a child's computer privileges, for instance, you may have already yelled at them, taken a toy away, tried bribing them, pleading with them. Punishment is a kind of acknowledgment that you have "lost a battle." It shows you were not able to negotiate your way to a better outcome. Discipline is very different. It involves a calm explanation of the behavior to be corrected, redirects a child to appropriate behavior, and rewards them for making a good behavioral choice.

Avoiding Blame

In the same way that blaming your child and attributing bad intentions to their actions is futile, so, too, is blaming others such as teachers and other children. Yes, it would be amazing if your child's teacher were a specialist in ADHD but their job is different. Most of the time, teachers have a sincere desire and commitment to making things easier for their students. They are not to blame for behaviors such as hyperactivity or inattentiveness, which can be part and parcel of ADHD.

Looking Out for the Positives

Instead of focusing on the more challenging behaviors your child may display, try to filter negativity so you can clearly view the things you most love about them. Criticism can harm a child's self-confidence, resilience, and motivation to learn and improve. Always be your child's biggest cheerleader and know that many of the behaviors that may annoy you are common at your child's age. Let your home be a haven for them.

Expecting Difficult Days

Some days will be worse than others, so make sure your expectations are realistic. At home, make sure your home is tidy and uncluttered, as disorganization can overwhelm children and reduce their ability to focus. Have a strategy ready for when things don't work out. If your child has an argument with their best friend, for instance, ask them to tell you about it when they are ready and help them put themselves in their friend's shoes, try to brainstorm how their friend may have felt, and come up with solutions on how to resolve the conflict positively.

Teaching by Example

Your children will have the best chance of finding their way through life's toughest challenges if they have good role models at home. Stay positive even when you have setbacks, set new goals to achieve when one falls by the wayside, maintain a good sense of humor, and share your emotions with those you love. It is very important for your child to know that they can share their frustrations, wishes, victories, defeats, and secrets with you.

Leaning on Others

People who have a good social life and a small but reliable group of family members and friends have lower stress than those who face life's vicissitudes all by themselves. Give yourself a break once in a while, rely on trusted people to take over when you need an afternoon off to enjoy a meal out, and share your thoughts and emotions with people you trust.

Focus on What Your Child Can Achieve

Your child may not be the best basketball player at school, but their extroverted personality and passion for performance may make them a whiz on stage. They may struggle at math but create vivid, unique, appealing artwork. Whenever your child expresses sadness about not being great at something others are, recognize and accept their feelings. Don't try to repress negative emotions. Let them know you understand why they may be feeling frustrated or disappointed. Soothe them when they are low and when they regain their sense of self, let them know that everyone (including you) has unachieved goals, dreams that may not have come true, and experiences they still dream of having.

Let them know that "failure" really isn't something to feel bad about at all because often, it points out a new direction to take.

So many people started out wanting to be one thing and ended up excelling at something else. Famous actor Dwayne "The Rock" Johnson, for instance, dreamed of becoming a successful football player but when he was cut from his team early in his career, he decided to become a professional wrestler instead, making a name for himself and eventually becoming an A-list actor.

Trying Out Different Strategies

As a parent, it is important to keep up-to-date on new findings, therapies, and approaches to ADHD. Read various pieces of research but always trust your own instincts as well. Don't get stuck in one approach if you come across a new one you think you may like to try out or you discover a therapy or treatment that has proven to be successful in studies or among the people you know and trust.

Choosing a Winning Strategy

Set specific, measurable goals and choose strategies that work for your child. For instance, your aim may be to ensure your child does their homework after school. Choose strategies such as star charts, immediate rewards (such as playing a game your child loves after they finish their tasks), and relaxation techniques such as controlled breathing before they commence their tasks. Try to eliminate obstacles that stand in your way. Techniques you might like to try include removing TV screens from the living room and bedroom, cooking healthy Mediterranean-style meals at home with your kids, or attending a fun class like Zumba with your child.

Employing Positive Parenting Strategies

ADHD can be frustrating sometimes but it is never the result of a child's intention to hurt, embarrass, or annoy you. Positive parenting does not mean turning a blind eye to your child's behaviors—in fact, it is important to be realistic. ADHD can be a big challenge not only for yourself but also for your child's siblings (who may feel like all your attention is going to your child with ADHD). Embracing a positive frame of mind is vital if you wish to meet the challenges of ADHD successfully (Smith & Segal, 2021). Positive parenting involves a wide array of strategies, including:

- *Remaining calm and focused on the big picture and the ultimate goal, instead of on the particular challenge you are facing on a given day.*

- *Putting things into perspective and giving situations their due importance. As the old saying goes, "Don't make a mountain out of a molehill."*

- *Relying on laughter. It truly is the best medicine!*

- *Believing in your child's ability to grow, master techniques, and learn strategies that can help them control their behaviors. Many strategies take time and patience but, one day, they can "click" and life can become considerably easier.*

- *Exercising self-compassion. Be as kind to yourself as you are to the people you care about. Take a break once in a while, make sure to get daily exercise, and feed yourself a healthy diet to stay energetic and focused.*

- *Embracing daily routines and establishing rules. Because a child with ADHD can have trouble focusing, established routines will help them remember what to do and where to find things. Keep schedules as simple as possible and ensure your child's surroundings are well-organized.*
-
- *Setting important rules such as bathing and brushing teeth every day, doing homework before playing, and making the bed is important.*

- *Using positive rewards and consequences to keep your child focused on tasks and motivated to do chores well. You can use a reward chart to keep kids updated on their progress. For a child with ADHD, immediate rewards work better than those that come later.*

- *Giving your child consequences when they misbehave. If they have a tantrum, allow them to have a "time-out" and calmly suggest alternative behaviors for the next time a similar situation arises. Don't try to explain your point of view until your child is calm and ready to listen to you.*

- *Giving your child the opportunity to proactively battle stress. There are so many tried-and-tested, scientifically proven ways to reduce stress levels. These include spending time in nature, exercising, creating art, playing or listening to music, using relaxing essential oils like lavender, having a hug, and using relaxation or meditation recordings during bedtime.*

- *Feeding your child a healthy diet. Because children with ADHD can be impulsive, they may be inclined to snack at irregular hours. Stop them from bingeing on unhealthy foods by feeding them meals and snacks at regular intervals. Get rid of high-sugar and refined snacks and make healthy snacks available throughout the day*

- *Helping your child have a positive social life by signing them up for activities they love, organizing playdates with other parents, and speaking with your child honestly and lovingly about important steps they can take to build good friendships with other children.*

Try to choose positive, loving moments to teach your child a lesson or give them feedback so as to increase the chances of your child being receptive to what you are saying. Correcting a child in the heat of a moment or raising your voice at them while telling them what to do correctly may only make them nervous and anxious and they may shut out what you are saying, or simply shut down.

Starting on the 8-Step Program

In the next eight chapters, I will introduce you to the eight-step approach. Once you have found a health professional or team you trust to guide you along your journey, they may suggest this type of approach in conjunction with medication. In some cases (for instance, if your child has less severe symptoms) they may recommend a behavioral approach first.

The 8-Step Program involves:

1. Rewiring the Motor System
2. Fine-Tuning Sensory Processing
3. Promoting Self-Awareness and Accountability
4. Leveraging Metacognition Strategies
5. Reducing Sensory Overload
6. Cultivating Stronger Self-Esteem
7. Improving Family Dynamics
8. Shifting the Physical Environment to Fit Specific Needs

I hope my method helps your child as much as it did my son. When trying the steps out, know that some will work better with your child than others. Keep trying, for strategies that work today, may change tomorrow, and techniques that didn't work out the first day may hit the mark after a few tries. Trying and testing different methods is vital until you find the perfect fit for your child.

STEP ONE:
Hone Your Child's Motor Skills

Whenever my son Neil seemed particularly wound up after a long day at school, I found that suggesting something active for him to do like play ball in our backyard or go for a swim (as opposed to trying to get him to rest) worked wonders. As time went by, I realized that exercise, dance, and other physical activities were Neil's way of releasing pent-up energy. In this chapter, I chose to share the games that Neil loved the most. They are all centered on enhancing children's motor skills.

Why Work on Motor Function?

A study by academics from the organization, Children and Adults with Attention-Deficit/Hyperactivity Disorder (CHADD) found that children with ADHD become more physically active when they are given a difficult task to complete than when they are asked to complete easier ones.

Additional research has found that children with ADHD perform better at set tasks after they have taken part in physical activity and if they are permitted a break or recess.

They also show an enhanced working memory task performance when they have higher rates of physical movement. Interestingly, this is not the case for children who do not have ADHD. The findings are a wake-up call to the importance that movement can have on your child's performance and well-being.

In the CHADD study, the researchers recruited 44 children aged ten to seventeen, some twenty-six of which had ADHD. The children wore fitness trackers on their ankles that measured how often and how intensely they engaged in movement. The children were asked to play a computer game to measure their attentiveness and cognitive control. The game involved pressing a specific key depending on whether an arrow moved left or right. An additional challenge was presented in the form of arrows that children were asked to ignore. The results showed that children with ADHD moved more frequently and intensely during the game than the control group. Moreover, their accuracy rates were higher while they were moving. This was not the same for the control group.

Children with ADHD find it hard to "sit still" while they are learning. It is important to recognize and find ways to allow children to move instead of punishing them for doing so. Teachers can also think of ways to incorporate activities that involve movement into classes, allowing for activity breaks and encouraging children to try out yoga, Pilates, jumping jacks, or other exercises between tasks.

Teachers should also allow children to use fidget toys in class instead of scolding them for moving their hands or holding, tearing, or squeezing items. Useful toys for children with ADHD range from elastic bands placed beneath desks to squishy balls kids can use while carrying out tasks. They should also enable children to move their legs beneath their chairs if they need to, finding ways to minimize noise so that other children are not distracted. Non-slip furniture pads can be used, for instance, or a small rug can be placed beneath a child's chair, to drown out noise.

The CHADD researchers mentioned that further research needed to be conducted to work out whether exercise breaks were as efficient as moving while carrying out a task. Interestingly, CHADD is not the only institution that has demonstrated the utility of movement. In the UK, Monkseaton High School conducted neuroscientific research and developed a system called "spaced learning" (Kellaway, 2010). The latter involves teaching children subject matter in one hour study sessions, dividing content into three "inputs" presented on PowerPoint. In between each input, children take ten-minute breaks and move, taking part in activities like basketball, juggling, or artistic creation. During the first input, information is presented. During the second, the presentation contains missing keywords children need to fill in. During the third input, children work on a task utilizing the information they have learned.

The results showed that children can retain an impressive amount of information this way.

This is because the brain creates long-term memories via pathways of individual cells that are switched on before connecting to other cells. In order to switch these cells on, breaks are necessary. Without a doubt, teachers of children with ADHD would benefit from trying out this and other systems that incorporate both breaks and movement in everyday lessons.

Similar bodies of research also reveal the importance of trying new things out, keeping an open mind, and trying to adapt classes to students' needs instead of forcing things to go the other way around. One is reminded of the following words of British educationalist, Stephen Heppell (Blunt, 2009): *"When teachers do things differently, the alternative is always better and more successful than traditional methods, because the earlier model of education wasn't built around the best way children can learn, but the best way to organize learning."*

Upping the Fun Factor

Neuroscientist, Judy Willis, hit the nail on the head when she said (Willis, 2007), "When we scrub joy and comfort from the classroom, we distance our students from effective information processing and long-term memory storage." Neuroimaging studies indicate that when students are comfortable, they can retain information and transmit it more efficiently. Fun, stress-free lessons also enable information to flow through the affective filter in the amygdala (the part of the brain responsible for emotional behavior and motivation), so children can understand new facts, make vital connections between different ideas, and come up with creative thoughts and ideas.

Improving Motor Skills Is Particularly Beneficial to Children with ADHD

A recent study (Jeyanthi et al., 2021) has shown that exercise helps children with ADHD improve their motor skills, physical fitness, and attention. It also helps them manage their issues and integrate with their peers at school and in social settings. The study involved a set exercise program lasting forty-five minutes. Children followed this program for a total of eighteen sessions, which took place over a period of six weeks. Not only did the participants enjoy major benefits in many areas but they also had fun while doing so. The researchers concluded that exercise should be considered (in addition to other forms of treatment and/or therapy) as an essential approach for reducing ADHD-related problems.

Games to Improve Motor Skills

There are so many fun ways to hone your child's gross motor skills (Kids at Max, n.d.). This set of skills includes components such as balance, coordination, muscle endurance, body awareness, weight shifting, coordination, climbing stairs, peddling a bike, and more. You can try out many different types of games and the good news is that there are so many available that your child will surely make their own list of favorites in no time. You should also work on improving fine motor skills—those which involve making movements using the small muscles in the hands and wrists. Your child might benefit from the following:

- ***Body awareness games.***
- ***Balance and coordination games.***

There are various means of honing one's balance and coordination, ranging from walking along a log or balance beam right through to playing the piano. Try teaching your child to juggle, play balloon-tossing games (trying to toss the balloon while completing the alphabet), and jump rope. The latter may seem simple but for young kids, it can actually be quite challenging to synchronize their hand and eye movements

- ***Fine motor exercises.***

To improve fine motor skills, try activities that involve drawing; using a keyboard; or using tools such as scissors, rulers, and molds. To make it fun, time how fast the whole family can untie and tie shoelaces, create play dough and putty figures, and play "rice races" by giving all players tweezers and seeing who can transfer a specific weight of rice grains from one bowl into another. If the grains are too small for your child, try slightly bigger items like Fruit Loops.

- ***Simon Says or copycat games.***

These games are simple but they are always a big hit! One person carries out a series of actions that the others have to follow. When you are the "leader," make sure to carry out high energy movements like jumping jacks, burpees, squats, and other activities that will help your child pick up motor skills while also reducing stress levels

- **_Treasure hunt games._**

   Hide clues indoors and outdoors that will lead your child to a secret treasure or reward. Make sure that your child has to use skills such as climbing, crawling, and jumping to get to the clues.

- **_Obstacle course games._**

   You can set up a fun obstacle course in your backyard or indoors. For an outdoor setting, consider items such as tires, slip-and-slides (for the summertime), traffic cones, inflatable pools with poles placed across them that kids have to walk over, small "hurdles" for kids to jump over, and more. For indoor training, tie strings at various angles from one side of the living room to the other, asking your child to walk through the different shapes formed by the crisscrossed strings. Place furniture at various heights that children can walk up, crawl under, and jump down from. Make sure that there is a soft source of support (a carpet, rug, or beanbag) for children to land on if they should fall.

One of the best things about the movement and indeed physical activity as a whole is its ability to engage and entertain everyone taking part. Activities involving movement will seem much less like work for your child with ADHD—something that is important when you consider that your child may already be attending other types of therapy such as behavioral therapy, which may be a little less "rough-and-tumble" than the games they naturally love.

Building, Planning, and Sequencing Skills

In order to boost your child's motor abilities, working on their planning and sequencing skills can help. To carry out even a seemingly simple movement (such as lifting a glass), the brain has to first plan what to do then work out how to do it so the muscles can see the action through. In children with motor planning issues, there can be a miscommunication between the sensory and motor systems (this miscommunication is called dyspraxia). If so, therapy will most probably be required. In therapy for dyspraxia, children learn how to break tasks into smaller, more achievable steps, repeat a set of steps to achieve their goal, build muscle strength, repeat instructions verbally, and much more.

See a health professional if your child shows signs of poor motor planning skills. Typical signs include having a lack of coordination, finding it difficult to complete multi-step instructions, and taking a longer than usual time to pick up new motor skills (Lumiere, 2019).

STEP TWO:
Help Your Child Modulate Their Response to Sensory Stimulation

ADHD and sensory issues can occur simultaneously and interact with each other. Sensory processing disorders are impairments in the way people people respond to sensory stimuli. There are two main types of sensory problems. The first is sensory over-responsivity or hypersensitivity and the second is under-responsivity. In sensory hypersensitivity, people respond to sensory stimuli in a more intense, longer, or quicker manner than usual. For instance, a child with over-responsivity might react strongly to having a cavity filled, close their ears when they hear music in the car, or cringe when you brush their hair. The sensations caused by these activities can be overwhelming and they may therefore avoid this type of experience.

Under-responsivity is said to be present when individuals are slow to respond to sensory input or are unaware of it altogether.

For instance, when watching an animation, it can be hard to see which character is voicing a sentence because there can be a large spatial difference between the origins of the sound and the visual information being received.

Children can also have a third form of sensory processing issue: they can be sensory seeking, craving sensory experiences. Sensory seekers may not have a suitable idea of personal space (for instance, they may get too physically close to others), walk with loud steps, enjoy bumping into structures or people, prefer rough play, and chew on non-food items (Morin, n.d.).

Research has found that sensory issues are more common in children who have ADHD (Ghanizadeh, 2011). In fact, it can sometimes be difficult to tell if your child has ADHD or sensory processing disorder (SPD) because around 40 percent of children who have symptoms of either ADHD or SPD have symptoms of both disorders. Sensory overload is actually a lot more prevalent than you might think—a 2004 study (Ahn et al., 2004) showed that around 5 percent of all kindergarten-aged children have sensory processing conditions.

Protecting Kids from Sensory Overload

The first step toward helping a child with hypersensitivity is to observe them so you can identify their triggers. Some children may be very sensitive to rough textures, while others may have no issues with the sense of touch but find loud noises (such as music, raised voices, or a dentist's drill) a source of anguish. Once you have identified these triggers, the following steps can help (Ivy Rehab Network, 2019):

Look for early signs of distress. Don't wait until your child is crying or angry. When you enter into a new environment, take a look at the aspects your child has trouble with—which could be lights that flash or are too bright or loud colors in a room's design. Try to eliminate the source of distress early. For instance, if you are in a bright room, try turning off a light. If a loud sound is coming from one side of your home or that of a neighbor, take your child to a quieter area.

Teach your child calming exercises. These can include deep breathing, listening to a song with earbuds, watching a relaxing video, reading a poem, or even going for a walk.

Give your child sensory toys or tools. These range from stress balls right through to buzzers, soft toys, or even a piece of soft fabric. Try to notice the items your child reaches for when they are stressed and make more of these items available at home, in their school bag, and when they visit friends.

Offer your child a weighted vest or blanket. There are a plethora of weighted items that can help soothe stress and anxiety. These include weighted vests and blankets. Their effect is similar to when one uses a swaddling blanket on a baby. The effect is one of protection and safety.

Encourage your child to play outside. Nature is a known de-stressing environment; one that appeals to the senses while also calming them. To motivate your child to head to your backyard when they are feeling a bit tense, create a child-friendly area that can include swings, a sandpit, a vegetable or herb garden, and the like.

Adopt a pet. Dogs and cats soothe stress and provide unconditional love and friendship.

Get to events early (before they are filled with people) so your child is not overwhelmed by too many sights and sounds. This way, you can leave early if necessary without having missed out completely on the experience.

Help your child plan their exit strategy. They should know what to do if they are at a friend's place, at a sports class, or at a camp and they begin to feel overwhelmed. Their strategy can involve leaving a room that has become too loud, calling you so you can pick them up, putting their earbuds on so they can listen to pleasant sounds and the like.

Ensure your home is tidy. Children with over-responsivity may have a deep aversion to messy surroundings. This is because their reaction to sensory input may be quite dramatic.

Follow a regular routine so your child will know what to expect. Use visual schedules and let your child know you will be doing something or going somewhere several minutes in advance.

To help your child with emotional regulation, use techniques like deep breathing, slow rocking, sitting on a beanbag, and the like. Kids who are feeling overwhelmed can also benefit from movements such as running and jumping, especially between activities in which they will be expected to sit.

Tips for Children with Under-Responsivity

Children with under-responsivity may not be into play, not notice people trying to get their attention, enjoy solitary activities, and seem a little indifferent to what is taking place around them (Star Institute, n.d.). They may not notice when they have been touched, be unable to perform tasks using their hands without watching their hands, and seem indifferent to colors, lights, or untidiness (very much in contrast to kids who have over-responsivity). To encourage your child to interact more with the world around them, try the following:

- **Use bright lights and moving** "pointer lights" that move across the ceiling.
- **Play loud, vibrant music** without a set rhythm.
- **Stimulate their sense of smell** with essential oils like peppermint, orange, or lemon. Your child may also enjoy wearing an aroma bracelet or having an essential oil diffuser in their room.
- **Encourage movement** (running, jumping jacks, burpees) before and after sitting activities (this piece of advice also works for those with over-sensitivity as it serves as a "break" between activities or states of mind).
- **Ask your child to accompany you when you walk your dog.** This will encourage them to notice the sights, sounds, and textures around them. Point these out, inviting them to listen to the crunch of leaves beneath their feet or the birdsong in the trees. Ask them to touch leaves, bark, and soft flowers.
- **Provide them with tools that will help them hone their motor skills.** Think glitter pens; scented markers; and brightly colored pens, pencils, and crayons.

Tips for Sensory-Seeking Children

For children who are strongly attracted to sensory stimuli, the main challenge can be to help them clear their minds, focus, and relax. When your child comes home, help them chill out in the following ways (Danneman, 2021):

- **Design a chill-out space for them.** This space should be quiet, uncluttered, and simply designed with items like a soft bean bag, soothing lighting, and a weighted blanket.
- **Design a movement zone.** Find another spot in your home that can also be used by others when your child does not need it. This space should ideally have a rocking chair or swing since swinging motions have a calming effect on the brain. Trapeze bar swings are ideal because the user has to "push" forward and pull inward, using strong motions to obtain desired height. As such, your child can also let go of pent-up energy while reaching a state of greater relaxation.
- **Give your child crunchy snacks** (crudites are ideal because they are so healthy) as they will love chewing and crunching away.
- **Give your child stress balls** and other items they can fidget with while doing work.
- **Create an obstacle course in your backyard or indoors in a large, empty space.** Features to include are tires, tables to jump over or crawl under, monkey bars, slides, and more

Children with sensory issues can have trouble receiving and responding to information received through their senses. Some can show over-responsive or under-responsive traits. Those with over-responsivity are most likely to have tantrums, cry, or strike things because they can feel so overwhelmed by stimuli they cannot control.

Those who are under-responsive, meanwhile, are often quiet and solitary but as they grow older, their under-responsiveness may make it harder for them to get excited about making new friends and taking part in learning activities. Yet others can show sensory seeking behaviors, being strongly attracted to sounds, textures, tastes, and vivid sights.

As a parent, it is important to know your child and to make a myriad of small but powerful changes that can bring out the best in your child and help them interact in a positive way with their surroundings.

https://vivianfoster.com

STEP THREE:
Teach Your Child Self-Awareness and Accountability

You cannot make changes to your behavior if you are unaware of what you are doing and how your actions are perceived by others. Self-awareness is a key skill that children need in order to achieve their personal goals, make friends with others, and gain self-confidence. Once your child has grown in this respect, they can learn the importance of taking accountability or "owning" their behaviors, making key changes that will lead to more positive outcomes.

Changing Behaviors You Know Don't Serve You

Hoping things will change on their own is a strategy that is bound to be unfruitful. When you think back on your own life, you may recall times in which you received feedback from your friends, spouse, or kids.

Negative feedback may have made you feel a little defensive at first. However, after a few hours, a day, or even a week went by, you may have realized that much of what your loved ones, colleagues, or acquaintances told you, was right. Perhaps you do tend to raise your voice when you are stressed at work, hang up the phone in the middle of an argument, or give instructions impatiently when others don't get it right on their first go. It is only when you become aware of these behaviors that you can commit to improving them.

For instance, you may decide to read up on anger management or see a therapist, resolve to never end a phone call by hanging up angrily, or commit to explaining things calmly until someone "gets" what you are trying to say.

Honesty Is a Gift

Children with ADHD need to be aware of the things that can potentially distance themselves from their goals and from others. As your child gets old enough to understand ADHD, you can begin to provide them with information about their disorder and genetics, your family history, behaviors involving impulsivity, and hyperactivity, and how these can be perceived by others. Your child should know that they are a unique combination of personality traits, family patterns, environments, schooling, and many more components in addition to ADHD. Tell them that being aware of their impulsiveness or hyperactivity is a positive thing because it can help them "check themselves" when working with others.

Being honest with your children and encouraging them to know themselves and work on changing things when required implies embracing a growth mentality. We are not fixed individuals; we can improve the things we do not like, but first, we have to be confident (and love ourselves) enough to accept ourselves without judgment. Self-awareness is ultimately the product of love.

Doing It Your Way

Making changes based on self-knowledge allows one to set realistic goals. For instance, if your child has difficulties finishing all their homework on time and they set themselves a very strict schedule (for instance, all homework must be completed by Friday afternoon at 5 p.m.), they may start out OK but end up feeling overwhelmed by pressure and burning out. Instead, it might be more profitable to space their end-of-week homework between Friday and Saturday morning, giving themselves a break to do anything they like after around 5 p.m. on Friday.

To set realistic goals, you need to know the extent to which you can push yourself. Therefore, if you and your child try something that proves to be too burdensome, switch it up, lighten it up, try a whole new strategy if necessary, but always try to base your plans on your child's authentic abilities and interests.

Tempering Self-Awareness with Self-Acceptance

Children with ADHD can sometimes be scared to accept themselves as they are, because all their lives they may have felt that they were letting someone down—their parents, teachers, and friends. They may associate self-acceptance with letting people down and allowing potentially detrimental behaviors to go unchecked. However, constantly living in fear of what others think will only stand in the way of their goals. It will be almost impossible to stick to a plan if they are constantly giving themselves negative messages and trying to conform to unrealistic expectations. Your child cannot authentically grow if they spend all their energy trying to be somebody else.

For a child with ADHD, self-acceptance does not have to mean not trying. It simply means accepting that some tasks and situations may be more difficult and making a plan to achieve improvement while also being true to oneself first and foremost. Being yourself as a child with ADHD simply means that you can stop fighting against yourself (Frank, 2019).

All Children Can Struggle with Self-Awareness

When you think back on your own life, you may recall how you were as a child or teen and you may laughingly "cringe" at some behaviors. Things you thought were OK back then may seem unacceptable to you now and that is only logical. All children can struggle with self-awareness.

Their brain is developing and they lack the experience required to teach them what is right and what is wrong in a myriad of settings. Don't expect your child with ADHD to be any more self-aware than you were at their age. Praise them when they do manage to "step outside themselves" and demonstrate an understanding of how their behaviors can affect themselves and others.

Teaching Self-Awareness

Self-awareness begins with asking oneself the right questions. However, your choice of language matters. Avoid asking your child with ADHD questions beginning with the word "Why." Instead of asking, "Why did you suddenly run away when you were starting to do your homework?" ask them "What" questions such as "What did you do just now after you sat to do your homework?" Then ask them the consequences of that action, "What happened to the work you were doing when you ran to the garden?" When they realize that if they get up very often, their written task will not get done in time for dinner, sit with them and patiently work out a few useful alternatives. For instance, "What about if you take a break every ten minutes, do ten jumping jacks or go on your swing for five minutes, then come back to your homework? Look, we can use this timer to make sure our study times and break times are scheduled." Children should be able to identify the consequences of different decisions (Low, 2021).

Be calm and model the behaviors you are trying to teach your child. If you want these strategies to "sink in," maintain a calm attitude, use humor, and be affectionate. Your child will look forward to this time with you instead of feeling like they have been reprimanded.

The Importance of Accountability

Once your child "owns" the consequences of their behavior, they will feel liberated. No longer will they have to feel shame, regret, or guilt. Being accountable means "doing what you say you are going to do on your own (or with help if you need it), being responsible for your actions, following rules, and managing your emotions properly" (Dixon, 2018).

Author and doctor Russell Barkley suggests a practical way to help your child become more self-aware: recording them on a smartphone (with their prior approval, of course) or camera. This technique is often used to promote social awareness in children with ASD but it can also work well for children and teens with ADHD.

You don't have to show a recording right away, "when the iron is hot." Instead, you can do so a few days down the line. Typical situations that will suit video recording include moments in which your child is interacting with others at the park, playing with siblings at home, or working on a homework task. A recording is a very real, objective means for your child to see, for instance, how many times they stopped a task or whether or not they waited their turn while playing with others.

It is an invaluable source of self-learning but of course, it should not be used if children feel it is obtrusive. You can also use bedtime (or times when you are alone with your child, such as when you are in the car together) to talk about your child's day and its major events—ask them to tell you both the favorite and most challenging parts of their day. If they tell you they had a hard time in class or while playing, once again use "what" questions, come up with alternatives, and get your child to commit to trying out one or more strategies. Always ask them to report back to you with their successes and "failures."

Ultimately, teach them that a so-called "failure" is simply an opportunity to grow and become a better person. All of us have "failures" but what marks a courageous person is being accountable for them and using them to make necessary self-improvements.

Be Your Child's Accountability Partner

Adults with ADHD are often advised to have an "accountability partner" at work. The latter helps them with self-awareness and time management. You can be this person for your child at home, giving them important pointers for their school and social life. You can help them with specific goals such as homework and routines and they will feel confident knowing that you are their teammate and that means you have their back, no matter what.

Practical Ways to Promote Accountability

To be the best accountability coach for your child, put a few practical plans into action. These include breaking down big tasks into smaller ones, setting a specific amount of time for each task, giving consequences for unfinished tasks, and setting realistic targets. Make sure not to frame consequences as a punishment.

For instance, your child may have to finish three homework tasks before being allowed to watch their favorite cartoon. If they do not do their work, the consequence is that there will no longer be enough time to watch the show they wanted to. Put a positive spin on the situation by saying, "We still have an hour. If you get it done by then there will be enough time to watch your show before dinner."

Finally, make sure the goals you are setting are achievable. If your child is aged ten, keep in mind that their executive function may correspond to that of a child aged seven (Wexelblatt, 2020). Don't expect more from your child than they can reasonably give, for judgment stunts the growth mindset and leads a child to judge rather than accept themselves.

STEP FOUR:
Teach Your Child Metacognition Strategies

In this chapter, parents will be given advice on how to improve metacognition (the awareness and understanding of their own thought processes). Metacognition is the ability to "think about thinking" or "know about knowing." It can help your child understand what drives their thoughts, feelings, and behaviors. Armed with this deeper knowledge about themselves they can step back and "observe themselves from afar" to understand what they are doing, how they are doing it, and how others are reacting to them.

Why Is Metacognition Important?

Children who adopt metacognitive strategies as part of their learning become more self-reliant, flexible, and productive. They learn to evaluate different options, particularly when there is more than one possible solution or course of action. In recent years, teachers have increasingly adapted their classes so as to encourage children to reflect on how they learn. Doing so can help students become better learners.

For instance, a child may find that they are distracted when working in class but that working in a quiet library is a big boon to their concentration and ability to retain information. By understanding how they learn, they can adapt their strategies and choose winning combinations (this combination may involve a specific place, time, memorization strategy, and more). Research indicates that the largest growth in metacognitive ability occurs between the ages of twelve and fifteen (Price-Mitchell, 2015). When teachers and parents cultivate the metacognitive approach to learning, children have a heightened ability to weigh up different choices and evaluate options, giving them the tools, they need to reflect both on their academic and personal lives.

Metacognition can also help children feel more positive about learning. When they come across a difficult math problem, for instance, they can say, "That's way too difficult. I just can't do it." The more suitable alternative is to use metacognitive skills and ask themselves questions like, "How can I overcome this obstacle?" "What if I search for this problem online?" "What is this area of math called? If I can identify it, I can look at how similar problems were solved in my book or online." Children need to know what is getting them stuck so they can find a solution that will clarify their doubts.

The Link Between Metacognition and Academic Performance

Metacognition encourages children to know themselves as learners and provides them with the skills they need to monitor themselves and regulate their cognitive processes. It helps them achieve academic success via five key aspects (Schraw & Dennison, 1994):

- **Planning**—Setting goals and organizing resources before studying.
- **Information management strategies**—Strategies for learning such as summarizing, selective focusing, using mind maps, and more.
- **Comprehension monitoring**—Assessing one's learning.
- **Debugging strategies**—Employing strategies to correct comprehension and performance errors.
- **Evaluation**—Analyzing one's performance and strategies to see if they have been effective.

All these approaches can help make one a better, more analytical student that does not just learn about new subjects, but also gleans vital insight into the way they think and learn. Metacognition skills are strongly linked to success in reading, writing, science, and math.

What Are the Elements of Metacognition?

The word "metacognition" was first used by Swiss psychologist Jean Piaget's American disciple, John Flavell of Stanford University, in the 1970s. Early theorists determined that metacognition is made up of four basic elements (Jax, n.d.).

The Metacognitive Environment: Piaget believed that it was important to let children talk about what they were doing, make mistakes and revisions, and make multiple attempts at something until they recognize their own patterns. A metacognitive environment enables children to be more self-aware and to adapt their learning strategies to achieve desired outcomes.

Awareness of Knowledge: Before children can understand and analyze what they are thinking, they need to be aware that they have knowledge. Parents can demonstrate this by asking their children, "What was Terabithia?" "What did Bilbo steal from Gollum?" or "How many yellow sticks did you count?" When children provide their answers, they become aware that they have processed information they can then discuss, talk, and debate about.

Awareness of Thinking: Lead by example, showing that you analyze your own thought processes. Start your sentences with phrases like "I was just thinking..." You might say, "I was just thinking that science is a lot more fun to learn when we do experiments." Also, start discussions about what characters from the books they are reading or the series/cartoons they are watching might be thinking. You might ask, "Why do you think Leslie decided to go to Terabithia when it was raining?"

Awareness of Strategies: Build on your child's previously acquired knowledge to predict outcomes and make decisions. For instance, you might ask, "What happened the last time we mixed baking soda with red vinegar?" or "Do you think it might be a good idea to use this glass or should we use a larger one?" When children realize that past learning can help them make sense of new learning activities, they will be able to grasp the importance of strategic learning.

Strategies for Enhancing Metacognition in Your Child

Thinking about thinking is a fun exercise, especially for curious parents and kids. Just a few strategies that may work well with your child include (Jacobson, n.d.):

> **Asking open-ended questions.** For instance, your child may say something like, "I think the book was boring." You can ask a question like, "Can you tell me why you think that? What aspects of the book made you feel bored?"
>
> **Encouraging children to know their triggers.** If your child is upset with their sibling, wait until they have cooled down a bit and ask them questions like, "Why do you think you got so annoyed when Billy told you that he was still using his tablet and you would have to wait?"

Encouraging solutions-based thinking. Wallowing in problems does nobody any good. While recognizing and accepting all emotions—including negative ones—is important, so, too, is knowing when to move on and focus on solutions. It's all about being proactive instead of reactive. Thus, you might ask your child, "How do you think you can handle having to wait to play next time?" It can be very empowering for your child to know that they actually have options; that they can do so much more than react to something that upsets or annoys them. Solutions-based thinking puts your child in control and helps raise their self-confidence. It avoids shame and blame and focuses on practical ways to improve future outcomes.

Asking process-oriented questions. Ask your child questions that will help them to understand how their learning process works. For instance, if they are writing a story, ask them how they will know that they have finished

Identifying obstacles. If your child is struggling with a task, ask them "What do you think it is about this task that is proving to be a stumbling block?" "How did you get past this obstacle the last time?" You might also say, "If you haven't tackled a problem like this before, let's brainstorm a few solutions so you can get past it and continue your essay."

Asking your child what they learned. Whether your child has had to summarize a text, do math homework, or make a graph for science, ask them what the task taught them. "What did you learn by doing your science homework that you didn't know before?"

Encouraging your child to keep a journal. Children who enjoy writing or keeping a diary or journal can benefit greatly from answering a few metacognitive questions every week. Questions can include "What did I enjoy learning most about this week?" "What things did I get stuck on this week?" "What strategies from the past enabled me to overcome new challenges?" "What study strategies helped me learn?" or "What strategies do I need to improve on next week?"

Talking about important things. If the drive to your child's school is long or you enjoy having a good chat with them on weekends, take special moments to talk about ideas and things that matter. Topics you might enjoy talking about once kids are mature enough to do so include the state of the environment, ethical fashion, wealth, justice, freedom, and the like.

Be Patient

Metacognition involves higher-order thinking and can take time to learn. Don't expect your child to be excited about ideas, thought processes, and learning strategies from the get-go.

Think of metacognition like a glass of water that you can fill day by day, drop by drop. A child in preschool can already begin to think about what activities they like and why, a school-aged child can easily discuss the types of tasks they find most difficult and come up with a pool of useful strategies with your help, and a teen can really start understanding their strengths and weaknesses and how to battle their biggest challenges with tried-and-tested strategies. By being patient with your child, you will be modeling useful behaviors they can adopt both now and when they are adults.

Studies have shown that impatience in adults is a strong predictor of factors such as credit card borrowing, spending on alcohol and tobacco, savings, and more. Patience enables your child to take a long-term view of things, to sacrifice impulse for a long-term reward, and to make decisions that will be good for their health and well-being in the long run. Everything that is worthwhile in life—ranging from academic success to friendships and relationships—necessitates looking to the future and making necessary sacrifices. Whenever you embark on any strategy alongside your child, giving them time to mature, learn the strategy, and apply it is vital if you want your child to be open to your involvement and excited about the new ideas and plans you come up with together.

STEP FIVE:
Help Your Child Make Sense of Sights and Sounds

Now it is time to help your child develop their ability to organize and make sense of what they see and hear. To do so, it helps to know about visual-spatial thinking, which can be defined as the ability to perceive visual information in one's environment, to represent it internally, integrate it with other experiences and senses, obtain meaning and understanding, and manipulate and transform these perceptions (Dimensions Foundation, 2005).

People who are highly skilled at visual-spatial learning are more attentive to their environment. They observe and appreciate the small details that make life and learning so special—such as the kind of plants growing in their neighborhood, the layout of their school, design features of architecture and interiors, and the like.

Visual-Spatial Skills

Visual-spatial skills are important (Kelly, n.d.). because they enable people to carry out a variety of tasks including following a map, parking their car in a tight spot, or catching a ball. Children use these processing skills to walk into a room without bumping into others, tie their shoes, and read. Children need visual-spatial skills, for instance, to differentiate between letters and numbers (such as "w" and "m," "p" and "b," or "3" and "8"). So many subjects require children to process and transform what they see—including math, English, and science. They are additionally required for sports, making one's way through mazes, and indeed almost every activity that depends on the sense of sight.

Visual-spatial skills are also involved in visual-spatial memory, which allows children to visualize something and retain this image in their minds. This type of memory is required to carry out mathematical problems, remember patterns and formulae, solve problems, make decisions, read, and recall specific images they may need to answer test questions correctly.

Another important component of working memory is the auditory-verbal storage system, which maintains linguistic information. Deficits in this system can result in problems with language acquisition, word decoding, and vocabulary acquisition. When either visual-spatial or auditory-verbal skills are lacking, it can be difficult to process information.

Working Memory and ADHD

Analytical studies have shown that children with ADHD can have both auditory-verbal and visual-spatial working memory impairments, independent of their intelligence and academic achievements (Shiels et al., 2008). The largest deficits seem to be in visual-spatial skills. The good news for parents is that both stimulant medication and behavioral interventions have been found to improve working memory in children with ADHD. Positive reinforcement is a particularly useful behavioral approach, with evidence indicating that "a high intensity of reinforcement is highly effective in ADHD." When your child performs a task well, pays attention, or follows your instructions, give them immediate rather than delayed rewards. Shiels et al. (2008) state that stimulant medication and incentives seem to enhance different components of visual-spatial working memory.

Shiels concludes that "it seems plausible that the combination of stimulant medication and incentives would result in the greatest overall improvement in visual-spatial working memory in children with ADHD."

Auditory-Verbal Issues

Children with ADHD may have trouble listening or understanding verbal information and, in some cases, their poor performance at school or in social settings may be related to auditory processing disorder (APD)— a "glitch" in the brain's ability to filter and process sounds and words (Scherer, 2021). Children with APD may have trouble filtering out sounds or distinguishing between similar sounds ("ba" and "ma," for instance).

Studies show that around 50 percent of children with ADHD may also have APD, though the latter can exist on its own, without ADHD. Symptoms of APD may include sound discrimination issues, having difficulties with memorizing information, and being confused when reading or telling stories.

If you suspect your child has APD, they should undergo testing with an audiologist when they are around six or seven years old. If APD is diagnosed, your child will need to work with a speech and language therapist to sharpen auditory memory, learn to differentiate sounds, and improve their language processing abilities. At home, you can help by conversing with your child when the background is silent, speaking slowly and using simple sentences, making sure your child is looking at you and paying attention before you speak, and asking them to repeat any words you have said that they do not understand.

Stepping into Your Child's Shoes

By now it is easy to see that a child with ADHD can have both visual-spatial and auditory-verbal issues that can interfere with the way they learn and interact with others. These components of working memory have solutions that can enhance key skills—including behavioral treatment. Your patience and effort are just as important. As mentioned above, being aware of how your child's working memory functions can help you take key steps toward making things easier for them.

When you feel like you have come to a standstill or you are having a particularly hard time getting through to your child, step back, pause, and exercise empathy. Think of what it might be like to be inside your child's mind and understand the reasons why they might feel frustrated or overwhelmed.

Children with ADHD can be frustrated when they are expected to learn, complete tasks, and communicate with others. They can find it hard to regulate their emotions and have difficulty with tasks calling for executive function skills such as working memory, flexible thinking, and self-control and inhibition (Understood Team, n.d.). This means that they may find it harder than you might to prioritize tasks or remember details. They can also take a little longer to mature developmentally. Every child matures at their own rate. As such, some children with ADHD can be popular, charismatic, and extroverted. Others can face rejection from their peers, which can contribute to lower self-esteem (Low, 2021).

The spectrum of emotions felt by a child with ADHD is wide and can include disconnection, isolation, restlessness, feeling lost or out of control, or simply feeling overwhelmed by the demands placed on them. Children with hyperactivity can have a bigger gap in cognitive performance (compared to their peers) than those without it.

Sometimes, the aspects of ADHD your child may struggle with can be caused by the medication they are taking. Symptoms of stimulant medications can include anxiety, irritability, stomach pain, and headaches (to mention a few).

Common side effects of non-stimulants, meanwhile, can include fatigue, decreased appetite, and somnolence. As mentioned above, medication can play an important role in improving working memory. However, parents also need to be observant of their potential side effects, so that any treatment interfering with a child's quality of life is replaced.

Myth Busting

There is much misinformation surrounding the subject of ADHD and people around you who are not familiar with the disorder may believe myths such as those indicating that ADHD is a type of laziness, that your child will outgrow it, or that it isn't even a real condition. Take time to gently inform people that this is not the case and be on the lookout for signs that people around your child may be stigmatizing them.

A 2020 review in The ADHD Report showed that peers perceive classmates with ADHD to be less caring and more likely to get into trouble than others and that teachers perceived their academic performance in a less positive light. Parents, too, could fall prey to stigmatizing their child, engaging in criticism, and being irritable with their child. If this is the case for you, consider learning anger management techniques. Know your emotions and triggers, take a break when needed, and avoid yelling at your child. They may already be overwhelmed as it is. Wait until you are calm and try to address issues you can both work on, placing a positive light on the goals you can achieve together, as a team.

Helping Your Child Manage Their Condition

In addition to working closely with your child's teachers, therapists, and medical team, there are many useful strategies you can use to help your child feel less overwhelmed and more comfortable, accepted, and loved at home. These include using clear, simple words to communicate; following a set daily routine; organizing your child's things; providing rewards to your child; and maintaining a positive attitude around your child at all times.

Playing Sensory Games

Sensory play activates connections in the brain's pathway, enhancing a child's ability to learn and remember information. Stimulate your child's five senses by trying out games that stimulate different senses (Sanghera, 2017):

The Sense of Hearing

Design and print out a chart of sounds (bird songs, leaves under your child's feet, planes overhead, cars, and the like) and head outside, taking a walk to the park or a green area. Ask your child to tick the box next to each sound he or she hears.

The Sense of Smell

Take a set of therapeutic-grade essential oil roll-ons and practice guessing which oil they are! Good ideas include orange (which can energize you and your child), lavender (for calming), and peppermint (for concentration and alertness).

The Sense of Sight

Collect around twelve items and put them on a tray, covering them with a piece of paper or cardboard. Ask your child to write down as many items as they remember.

The Sense of Touch

Take turns blindfolding each other and putting items with different textures into each other's hands. Make it a messy, fun game using items like Jell-o, sand, clay, faux fur, leaves, a nail file, and indeed as many items with interesting textures as you can think of! If you don't have time to prepare, try the same activity in a green/forest area. There are always so many textures in the Great Outdoors, ranging from rough tree barks to smooth leaves, the taste of blueberries, and the earthy feel of soil.

The Sense of Taste

Blindfolding each other and tasting an array of treats is always loads of fun. When trying this game out, try to find one food for each primary taste sensation (sweet, sour, bitter, salty, and umami). Umami means "the essence of deliciousness" in Japanese and its taste is often described as meaty and earthy. Just a few umami foods to sample include mushrooms, aged cheeses, green tea, seaweeds, and soy foods.

STEP SIX:
Build Your Child's Self-Esteem

Studies have shown that children with ADHD can have lower scores on self-esteem domains compared to people with self-esteem (Mazzone et al., 2013). The domains of self-esteem vary depending on age, but in general, they cover areas such as academic, social, and athletic accomplishment, and appearance. Self-esteem can be defined as a person's cognitive and emotional concept about himself or herself. It can touch upon different areas—including achievement, competence, and self-worth.

Why Is Self-Esteem So Important for Children with ADHD?

All children have numerous expectations placed upon them from parents, teachers, family members, friends, and more. These vary depending on the context.

For instance, the rules that govern a classroom are very different from those a child may be expected to follow at a family member's home. Juggling all these expectations can be difficult for any child (since they are still maturing and learning about themselves and how to function in the world) yet for a child with ADHD, it can be overwhelming since they may have poor executive function control. This means that they may unwittingly blurt out their thoughts in class, rush to the front of a queue instead of waiting their turn or find it hard to focus when a classmate is talking about themselves. This can cause rejection and stigmatization.

Children with ADHD can be subjected to repeated criticism and correction from the people that make up their day-to-day life and this negativity can lead them to predict that they will fail again in the future. Clearly, the effect on their self-esteem is incomparable to what you or I might have experienced as a child. As reported by Thriving with ADHD (n.d.), by the time a child with ADHD reaches adulthood, they will have been exposed to "years of feeling demoralized, discouraged and ineffective because of a long-standing history of frustration and failures in school, work, family, social, and daily adaptive domains." Many will feel that they never lived up to what their talents and abilities could have led them to achieve.

Just think of a few statements your child may listen to every day of their life: "Stop fidgeting." "Concentrate!" "How many times do I have to remind you?" "You did it right last time."

Imagine the messages this leads children to tell themselves. These might be "I've had enough." "I'll never get it right." "I'm hopeless." "I'm useless."

Shame can lead a child to stop trying to achieve their full potential. It can make them angry and can cause them to lash out at themselves or at others. It can increase the risk of them adopting risky behaviors or of having anxiety or depression. As a parent, it is so important to work on helping them build healthy self-esteem.

Building Self-Esteem in Your Child

Research has shown that your parenting style and your child's self-esteem are inexorably linked. One parenting style—called "parental reflective functioning"(a learned and practiced skill) can be particularly useful when it comes to helping your child regulate their emotions, develop cognitive abilities, and form healthy social relationships (CHADD, 2017). This style involves recognizing, understanding, and accommodating how your child thinks and feels. For instance, if your child feels frustrated because they cannot do a homework task, instead of telling them "Just get on with it" or "Try harder" you should try to get inside their mind, understand the frustration they are feeling, proactively engage with them to promote self-confidence and use gentle language, humor, and even touch to let them know they are accepted, loved, and admire just as they are.

There are two important steps to take when practicing the skill of parental reflective functioning. First, praise your child for their accomplishments. Second, let them know you are aware of the challenges that made the task or activity difficult. Additional tips include:

- **Recognize small victories.** Remember that your child may receive an undue percentage of negative feedback from peers and other people. Counter this ratio by giving honest feedback when your child makes an effort and aces it!
- **Be specific.** Don't say something generic like, "Well done!" Instead, say, "Wow, you finished all that math homework and there were twenty algebra questions. That must have taken plenty of concentration."
- **State the challenges your child may have overcome to accomplish their goal.** You might say something like, "I know it can be hard to remember all the instructions for writing that paragraph but you followed what the teacher asked for and the result was so good."
- **Identify your child's positive traits.** Remember that children with ADHD have positive "mirror traits" of those they are usually criticized for. Take distractibility. The mirror of this trait might be curiosity (Kids in the House, n.d.). Think of impulsivity—its mirror could very well be creativity. As a parent, you know your child's strengths more than anyone. Remind them of

the things they shine in and give them all the tools and opportunities they need to make the most of these positive mirror traits.

- **Allow your child to relax when they first come home from school.** They may still be feeling a little anxious from academic demands. Let them know that downtime is important when they are stressed.
- **Don't use your child's favorite activity as punishment.** If your child fails to do a chore, for instance, don't stop them from drawing if they live and breathe for this activity. Remember that this may be the only outlet they have after a tough day.
- **Help your child break down big goals into smaller ones.** Congratulate them on each mini-goal achieved and try to teach them how to break down big tasks into smaller ones so they can do so on their own—for instance, when they are at school.
- **Practice role-playing strategies with your child.** Ask them to think of how their friend might feel if they were to pull a toy out of their friend's hand, talk when the friend was still speaking, or not wait their turn. Role-play a more positive behavior that their friend will most likely be much happier about.

- **Enjoy quality time with your child.** Slot in a little "we time" for just the two of you and use it to do something you both love. It could be enjoying time on the beach, going for a walk with the dog, or heading to your child's favorite restaurant for a weekend snack.
- **Let your child know that you love them just the way they are.** There are few things that can bolster self-esteem like knowing that someone will always have your back; that you don't need to be, do, or say something to be loved.
- **Consider parent training.** It will help you learn more positive strategies that your child will benefit from greatly both in the short and long term.
- **Build strong family connections.** Your child should ideally have a support system that extends beyond his family at home. Parents, aunts, grandparents, and cousins can all help them feel like they belong and that love is available from many different people.
- **Allow your child to shine.** We all love being successful at something. Foster your child's talents and abilities by providing them with materials and extra classes if they express a desire for it. Your child may be a whiz at theatrical performance, piano playing, or capoeira. Whatever it is, invest the time required to let your little star shine brightly.

Games That Foster Self-Esteem

Games are a wonderful way to teach children about the importance of self-esteem in a fun, engaging way. Because children with ADHD can find it difficult to focus, ensuring the activities are dynamic will increase the likelihood of them learning vital lessons. Just a few games to consider include geocaching (check out what the nearest state park has lined up, as many organize regular and seasonal events), "catching the compliment" (a group of people throw a ball around, complimenting the person they throw the ball to), and dice rolling (give the person as many compliments as the number on the dice).

Depending on your child's strength, you can choose activities they can excel at. For instance, if your child is creative, they may like to join you in creating a fun story you can write down and even illustrate. To spark a few ideas, give everyone around three cards, asking everyone to write a word or phrase on each card. You can then shuffle the cards and try to create a story incorporating everything that is written down on them. Another, easier way to brainstorm ideas is to ask everyone to choose three things from the house and bring them to a meeting point. You can then use these items to dream up a fantastical, memorable story. Don't forget to record the moment; it will probably be loads of fun to watch a few years down the road!

Mark's Story

Thus far, we have discussed six of the eight methods that can help bring out the best in a child with ADHD. One of the first children (apart from my son Neil) that I tried a few of the methods out on was Mark—an eight-year-old boy in my English class. I was a good friend of Mark's mom, Gemma, a mom of three who, at the time, was really struggling with her son's ADHD. Mark was hyperactive and I remember him finding it very difficult to sit down and pay attention in class. When I would ask the class to read, he would take his book and run in a square shape around all the children, some of whom would complain, get angry, and sometimes say cruel things to Mark.

As Mark's family lived one street down from my family, Gemma would often ask me over for coffee and Mark was always happy to see me. I remember being amazed that after the hard day he had had, he remained bubbly, affectionate, and enthusiastic. He used to hug me tightly and one Christmas, he wrote me a card saying I was his favorite teacher. The card had an absolutely wonderful drawing of myself, dressed in my favorite flowery dress and wearing my tortoiseshell glasses. I laughed and delighted at all the details he remembered to include. Mark has a loving family but sometimes they don't get it 100 percent right (we all have flaws and it takes time to know how to regulate one's own emotions while also helping a child regulate theirs). Gemma was a perfectionist and she just wanted everything to be "fixed," quickly.

Because my own son has ADHD, I gently shared my method with Gemma, who was keen on trying out new, different ways to help her son. I began by asking her to put herself in his shoes, to try to understand how hard it was to go through what he did in class (I gave her specific instances of others ostracizing or expecting too much of him), only to come home to parents who would get annoyed when he was unable to complete all his homework, do his chores, and get to bed in time.

I helped Gemma create a written schedule for Mark. This included half an hour of "me time" for him when he would get home from school. He could do whatever he wanted and he usually chose to play his favorite "building block" computer game. At a specific time, he was to do his homework. I explained the importance of breaking down homework into smaller chunks. For instance, if Mark was asked to read a passage and answer questions, it could help him to clearly define all the steps he needed to complete: 1. Read the pages the teacher suggested with her help. 2. Talk about possible answers and choose the one he thought was best. 3. Write the answers down.

Next up was dinner, a bath, then a little story time with Dad. As Mark settled into his routine, getting him to do chores or his homework became less of a "battle." I also encouraged Gemma to help Mark with emotional regulation. This began with labeling his emotions: "You must be scared," "Wow! You must feel frustrated." "It must be very hard to concentrate for so long to finish that task." Soon she learned to balance her perfectionism by celebrating Mark's small victories—which eventually became larger ones. She used games such as emotion-sorting games, calming yoga, and emotion flashcards to teach Mark how to talk about his feelings.

We also tried out various games aimed at strengthening Mark's self-esteem and these produced some of the best results imaginable. On some days we had fun delving into sensory activities; on others, we played body awareness or balancing games to strengthen his motor system.

Role-playing was a particularly powerful way for Mark to understand how his peers felt when he talked over them, ran around while they were trying to study, or pulled things out of their hands. He learned more positive outlets for tension and hyperactivity—just having a stress ball in class made it easier to wait his turn. I additionally encouraged his classmates to understand that Mark needed to move in order to learn. Some of them decided to join him and their results were surprisingly good! It seemed that a little movement could be positive for everyone, after all.

Gemma soon began to understand how much fun simply being with Mark was. On his ninth birthday, I remember her telling me how, of all the steps in the method, the one she enjoyed the most was putting herself in his shoes—for it was only then that she realized how strong and resilient he was.

STEP SEVEN:
Recognize and Eradicate Negative Family Patterns

Every family has its own patterns, which can be defined as characteristic behaviors, emotional tones, and attitudes of its members toward each other. Some families are very close, while others are more independent. Some embrace the company and presence of friends and family while others are more solitary. Family members can (and often do) repeat patterns (including problematic ones) from one generation to the next. The reasons are manifold (Poehlmann et al., 2003) and can include genetics, parenting styles, coping strategies, behavior modeling, and more.

Just a few problems that can be passed from people to their children and grandchildren include substance abuse, difficulties with anger management, neglect, and more. However, this cycle can be broken with the help of loving, supportive relationships, emotional support from others, and/or therapy.

For a child with ADHD, being in a loving, peaceful home can very much help them set and achieve goals. When they are supported and understood, it is easier for them to focus, work alongside accountability partners, and strive to be their best while knowing they are loved unconditionally. On the contrary, children who are raised by parents with behavioral issues caused by negative family patterns can have more behavioral issues, developmental problems, and learning and social issues.

If you had a difficult childhood—for instance, if you were in a home in which anger was allowed to go unchecked—you may benefit from therapies like cognitive-behavioral therapy, which highlights the important connection between how you think, feel, and behave. To work out whether or not you have negative family patterns you would like to break, ask yourself the following questions:

- What was my childhood like?
- How did my parents treat me?
- Did I feel loved and accepted or did I feel overly criticized, controlled, or neglected?
- Was there a lot of shouting in my home or did my parents use positive conflict resolution skills to communicate?
- What strengths did I gain by being part of my family when I was a child and what weaknesses may I have?
- Do I ever behave with my children in a way that my parents behaved with me? Is there any negative aspect to this behavior that I should work on?
- Do I have any other conditions—for instance, depression—that are standing in the way of my being the best parent to my child with ADHD?

If there are many negative family patterns that require addressing, therapy may help. If there are just one or two things you'd like to change and they are not severe (for instance, you may need to praise your child more or make quality time for them), then reading, analyzing aspects you need to change, strategizing, and trying out new behaviors can help.

Negative Statements to Avoid Saying to Your Child

One negative family pattern involves being over critical. Even on days when you feel like you're "at the end of your tether," you should avoid saying hurtful things to your child. For a child with ADHD, statements to be avoided include:

- **"Your ADHD isn't an excuse for your behavior."**

Your child can find it very hard to complete tasks and chores if focusing on work is a challenge. Even if they occasionally let you down, never mention their disorder when you are telling them they have done something wrong or asking them to complete a task.

- **"You can focus on computer games so you must be able to finish your homework as well."**

In reality, children with ADHD can hyperfocus on the things that fascinate them. Your child is not willfully being inattentive because homework is "boring." Quite simply, subjects that do not fascinate them are much harder to focus on.

- **"Don't tell anyone you have ADHD."**
Shame is one of the worst things you can teach a child. Telling them to hide their disorder is a way of putting them down or telling them they are not good enough as they are. Whether or not to share with others that they have ADHD should be their decision and theirs alone.

If you catch yourself with the urge to label your child or attribute qualities to them they may not have—be careful with clichés like "All kids with ADHD are creative." Think back to your own family patterns and analyze how you can break the cycle.

Behaviors to Avoid

Just a few things that can get in the way of good parenting include:

- **All-or-nothing, polarized thinking.** Always be open to new information, research, and advice from other parents who have children with ADHD. Every child is unique and has strategies that can work better and worse but they are also constantly changing and their needs may change as the weeks, months, or years pass.
- **Illogical thinking.** Try to base your decision on sound, logical ideas. Think long-term instead of finding quick solutions that will not benefit your child in the long run.
- **Blaming the other parent (if you are a two-parent family) or other family members.** Creating a culture of blame is a negative family pattern that will not only hurt your child in the present moment but also affect the way they interact with others in their adulthood.

Positive Actions to Take to Establish Healthy Family Habits

There are many different types of families and each involves unique ideas of how to bond, relax, and spend time together. Healthy habits involve a wide array of actions that can include:

- **Taking time to de-stress and relax.** Calm parents react better to challenging circumstances and situations. They see the "big picture" and understand that one bad day or one specific behavior does not define their child. De-stressing does not mean passively sitting on a sofa but rather, tackling stress proactively. There are a plethora of scientifically proven stress-busters, ranging from yoga right through to taking a "forest bath" (visiting a green area and opening your senses to the beauty around you).

- **Utilizing healthy conflict resolution skills.** This involves trying to defuse tension, listening to loved ones with a sincere intention to understand them, setting and respecting healthy boundaries, using "I" instead of "you" language, avoiding statements like "you always" or "you never," avoiding creating triangles within one's family, and more. Families can often benefit from therapy to improve conflict resolution skills if needed.

- **Taking time to choose the best solution.** As parents, it is important to show your children that sometimes problems require work, strategizing, and experimentation. Finding the easiest or quickest solution won't necessarily solve problems in the long run.

- **Working as a team.** Your whole family should work toward common goals. If you and your partner, spouse, or other significant family member are at constant loggerheads, an atmosphere of tension will be created that can worsen your child's behavior and start a cycle that is detrimental to their, and your, mental health.

- **Finding environments that contribute to your child's growth.** Within your home, there are many small changes you can make that will help your child unwind, de-stress, and relax.

Creating an ADHD-Friendly Home Atmosphere

Your home should ideally be a haven for your child (Low, 2021); one in which various targets are hit. Try to ensure your child's home environment contains the following elements:

- **An environment that promotes learning.**
  Your child should have access to a wide array of learning tools, toys, and materials, ranging from building blocks to paint, paper, accessories, and the like. Interesting books, materials on the subjects they are interested in, computers, and a desk where you can teach your child skills like how to map information or subdivide homework tasks, can all help your child achieve their academic goals.

- **A physical environment that helps your child concentrate and enjoy learning or taking part in their favorite activities.**

    Your child's workspace should be naturally lit and ideally have a view to a green space such as a garden or yard (unless your child has inattentive behaviors, in which case a window may not be the best idea). If you live in an urban setting, bring a few indoor plants into your living space to promote calm and focus.

Try to work out the aspects that promote better learning in your child. These can include providing healthy snacks between tasks, classical music, positive statements, the use of games while your child is doing chores or completing homework tasks, and of course, the presence of pets. A study by University of British Columbia Okanagan campus researchers (Rousseau & Tardif-Williams, 2019) showed that reading in the presence of a dog provides children with the motivation to read longer and persevere through more challenging passages. Dogs and cats can also lower stress levels and your child may enjoy "teaching" lessons to their dog, reading to them, or simply having their four-pawed friend close to them when they are working.

https://vivianfoster.com

STEP EIGHT:
Work on Your Child's Physical Health and Well-Being

A child's physical and mental health and well-being are intricately linked. Making improvements to your child's physical health can positively affect their mental health and well-being and reduce some of their symptoms. The final step in my method involves making your child's surroundings comfortable, ensuring they do not have any condition that can be causing them pain or discomfort, feeding them the fuel they need to be their most energetic and happiest selves, and making decisions on their use of electronics.

The Power of Observation

Be attentive to the environments your child is naturally drawn to. Some kids love being outside playing beneath the sun, or discovering new terrains in the woods. Others are more into the comfort of sitting by the fireside on their spot on the sofa in the company of their comfort blanket. In addition to using your powers of observation, ask your child questions about the things they love. Ask them what their favorite sport is, and why. Tell them to dream up an ideal day you two could spend together and break it down into its individual components. Join your child in discovering new environments and spend time with them in their usual nooks as well.

Stick to Your Child's Physical Health Calendar

Physical tests are recommended at specific stages. These vary according to age. For instance, infants see physicians at approximately two weeks, two months, four months, six months, nine months, and one year. Toddlers, meanwhile, usually see their doctor at one-and-a-half years, two years, and three years.

Children over the age of five only need to visit their pediatrician every two years more or less, as is the case for teenagers. Some tests need to be started very early—a child should have their first eye test, for instance, at about six months old, with a follow-up at the age of three and then again when they are five or six then, if they don't need glasses, every two years, more or less. Read up on recommended tests and make sure to comply with your child's schedule so you can take the opportunity to inquire about any behaviors you think could be related to physical issues.

The Importance of Sound Nutrition

Nutrition can impact everything from a child's mood to learning capacities. Research indicates, for instance, that excessive sugar intake could contribute to aggressive behaviors and classic ADHD-related behaviors (Johnson et al., 2021). Fructose—a component of sugar and high fructose corn syrup—and uric acid (which is produced when the body breaks down fructose) increase the risk of behavioral disorders. Fructose essentially lowers energy levels in cells and triggers a response in them which is similar to what happens when a person is ravenous. Behaviors such as impulsivity, rapid decision-making, aggressiveness, and the search for novel experiences can all increase.

The scientists also noted that fructose consumption has skyrocketed in recent years. This ingredient is present in a host of foods you may not imagine, both natural and refined— including agave syrup, honey, dried fruit, burgers, apple pies, sauces, salad dressings, and more. Sugar alone cannot be blamed for aggressive behavior but it can be a contributor to energy spikes and slumps and ensuing negative behaviors.

The topic of food additives and their effects on the behavior of kids with ADHD is controversial. Studies are divided; some indicate that certain food colorings and preservatives can promote hyperactivity, although the FDA Committee has determined that there is no proven link between food colorings and hyperactive behavior. As reported by the Mayo Clinic (Agerter, 2017), further research is required to is required to determine if food additives should be eliminated from children's diets. Of course, it is always a good idea to feed your child a healthy, Mediterranean diet that is low in refined sugar, and salty foods and that mainly comprises lean protein sources, healthy Omega-3 essential fatty acids, fresh fruits and vegetables, grains, pulses, and nuts.

Indoor Air Pollution and ADHD

In 2014, researchers from the Columbia Center for Children's Environmental Health at the Mailman School of Public Health (Perera et al., 2014) found that parental exposure to a component of air pollution called PAH raised the odds of childhood ADHD-related behavioral problems in children.

The researchers followed 233 non-smoking pregnant women and their children from pregnancy throughout childhood, finding that children whose mothers were exposed to PAH during pregnancy had a significantly higher number and degree of ADHD symptoms than children whose moms were not exposed to this compound.

The exact link between air pollution and behavior is not known, but scientists suspect that PAH may disrupt the endocrine system, cause oxidative stress and DNA damage, and interfere with placental growth factors, leading to a lower exchange of oxygen and nutrients. Another study (Newman et al., 2013) found that children exposed to traffic-related air pollution in their first year of life had higher hyperactivity scores at age seven.

Improving Your Indoor Air Quality

Items that can harm the quality of your indoor air include paraffin candles, harsh cleaning products, spray-on skincare and beauty products, carpets, and pressed-wood furniture. The latter, for instance, can contain formaldehyde (a material that is used to make glue, adhesives, some paints and coating products, and some clothing and curtains). Be careful of sofas that are over ten years old, as they may contain flame retardants, which are linked to reduced IQ, cancer, and hyperactivity (Weiss-Hills, 2018).

To improve the quality of your air at home, try steam vacuuming instead of using harsh products, consider replacing carpets with hardwood or other hard floorings, and replace sofas and soft furnishings that are old and may contain flame retardants.

Creating Comfort through Light and Sound

Pay attention to aspects such as light and sound, since lighting that is too bright and loud sounds from areas like the kitchen, living room, and spaces with home entertainment equipment may be overwhelming for your child. Dimming features in lighting can help you find the perfect level of brightness for your child to do their work without feeling overwhelmed. Sound-producing equipment should be turned off when your child is working on tasks involving concentration.

To ensure your child enjoys good sleep quality and quantity, fit their bedroom with blackout curtains and, if there is noise surrounding your home, invest in soundproofing. Ideal sleep conditions are dark, cool, and completely silent.

ADHD and the Use of Electronics

Like their parents, most kids these days can be quite reliant on electronic devices such as tablets, phones, and desktop computers. Indeed, some schools even incorporate the use of laptop computers in some or all subjects. Whether or not electronic use can be detrimental to children with ADHD (and indeed, all children) is very much a topic of debate. On the one hand, electronics provide children with access to information, learning apps, and video material that can make learning more engaging and fun.

On the other hand, some research—such as that published by the National Institute of Mental Health shows that extensive use of TV and video games can promote the development of brain systems that prioritize scanning and shifting attention at the expense of focusing (Jensen, 1997).

Another study by San Diego State University and University of Georgia scientists (Twenge et al., 2018)— which involved data obtained from surveys of 1.1million students from Grades 8, 10, and 12—found that on average, kids who spent more time using screen devices were less happy than those who spent time in non-screen related activities such as sports, reading, and in-person social interaction. Too much screen time is also linked to obesity and musculoskeletal and postural problems (children who lean forward while using their phones, for instance, can experience shoulder and neck discomfort and pain). In general, being too radical about screens vs. no screens may be futile as totally removing screens from your children's lives can make it hard for them to learn and even unwind if they enjoy an occasional game. You can try different strategies—for instance, only permitting your child to play on-screen games on weekends (for a specified amount of time).

Prohibiting screens radically can only make children more interested in them and older kids and teens can grow frustrated or angry if they feel like they are being over-controlled. Try and test different strategies and see what works best for your child.

https://vivianfoster.com

14

PROMOTING CALM, HEALTHY RELATIONSHIPS WITH PEERS

By following each of the steps in my eight-step method, you will hopefully have gone a long way toward promoting and rewarding positive behavior and reducing the triggers that can cause hyperactivity and other issues. Helping your child improve their social skills and make better connections with peers is also key, as friendship and support are important at every stage of life.

Allowing Your Child to Simply "Be"

Parents can love their children so much that they can try to protect them against possible hurt. While the desire to save children from pain is universal, you cannot live your life vicariously through your child, project your own wants and needs onto them, or expect them to conform to a social standard set by yourself or others. A child may have good social connections from their own perspective, so don't set expectations for them based on your own desires. Some children need to be surrounded by many friends to feel content, while others are more content to be part of a small group with shared interests, hobbies, or ways of seeing the world. If you notice your child is lonely or they tell you they wish they had a wider social circle, however, then it is a sign that they may need your help with honing their social skills. A few tips you may find useful (Mayo Clinic Health System, 2020) include:

- **Giving your child immediate feedback about inappropriate behavior.** Children with ADHD may find it hard to "read" the situation they are in and understand how they are being perceived by others. They can also act impulsively, without thinking about consequences. Help them work on behaviors that can stand in the way of making friendships. For instance, if they are swimming and they start shouting because other children are using a floaty toy they want, say something like, "Sandra, wait your turn, everyone is eager to use the floaty just like you so being patient is important."

- **Give immediate, frequent rewards for good behavior.**

- **Schedule playdates with one or two friends that your child feels safe and secure with.** Organizing big parties or going to crowded parks can make your child feel overwhelmed.

- **When scheduling playdates, choose activities your child is interested in and think about the amount of time you wish to stay, beforehand.** If you wish, let other parents know that you will only be staying for a specific amount of time.

- **Role-play the scenarios and situations your child needs help with.** Just a few skills you may like to focus on when taking part in role-playing activities include asking others about their thoughts and views, taking turns to talk, and showing interest in what other children are saying or doing (Low, 2021).

- **Focus on the areas your child is struggling the most with.** There is an old saying that goes, "Know which battles are worth fighting." If you criticize every little thing your child does, they can soon become desensitized to what you are saying and simply block out your words. Choose your words wisely and pick the right moment. Say what you need to simply, don't nag or repeat the same sentences, and give your child time to absorb and process what you have told them.

Middle School Friendships

As a child enters middle school, relationships can become a little more complicated, and this time can be even more challenging for children with ADHD—which is why you should continue to be interested in their social lives and continue to be their "friendship mentor."

Actively help your child build close relationships with kind, understanding children that love your child just as they are. Your child's best friend may live half an hour away but the drive may very well be worth it if this friendship gives meaning and happiness to your child's life. Bear in mind that middle and high school years can be tough and that children can become almost desperate to fit in with their peers. Even if a child has only one or two good friends, these relationships can be a powerful buffer against the pain of being ostracized by others.

Talk to other parents and do some research to find positive community groups that foster social skills and teach children a host of additional skills—outdoor youth programs, mountain trekking or biking groups, the Boy and Girl Scouts, sports teams, and environmental groups are just a few groups your child may want to join. Get to know the group organizers, teachers, activity leaders, coaches, and other individuals who head these groups, telling them about your child's interests and needs.

By being friends with the adults who play an important role in your child's life, you can discover vital information about your child you may not have known (including how they interact with others). The information you receive may be a wonderful surprise. You should also work closely with your child's teachers. Don't wait until an issue becomes so big you only find out about it in your child's report card. By maintaining a close relationship with teachers from the start, you can nip problems in the bud and work on behaviors while they are incipient.

If your child is struggling with schoolwork, their teacher should still find ways to bring positive attention to your child. They can do this by assigning special tasks or work to your child that brings out their talents and abilities. Talk to your child's teacher about changes that can be made to the physical environment to reduce distractions or enable a child to live with instead of struggling against their symptoms (Kids Health, 2020.). Strategies they might employ include praising your child's efforts, being positive and encouraging, giving clear and short instructions, seating a child in an area with fewer distractions, and teaching children how to "proof" their own work so they find mistakes and correct them before handing in their work.

Honing Flexibility

Teaching your child to be flexible can also help them adapt mentally to changing circumstances and challenges—and these often present themselves when making new friends and sustaining old ones. People with ADHD can find it inherently difficult to adapt quickly to new, unexpected situations but sometimes friends will change plans, interests, and activities and being open-minded to change is a good way to sustain relationships. Hone this quality by taking the following actions.

Show your child that you understand them.

When they are upset about a change, don't try to make them suppress or silence their feelings. Allow them to express their pain and let them know you would feel similarly if you were in their shoes. This will let them know you are on their side.

Explain that mental flexibility takes time.

Let them know why, throughout their lifetime, adapting to changes and unexpected demands is important. As much as human beings may try to control the events that surround them, they are constantly being called to display flexibility in areas such as work, relationships, and group activities. Let them know that although things may be difficult at first, they will get better at it because cognitive flexibility is a learned skill.

Help them regulate their emotions.

They should know how to label emotions like sadness, fear, anger, and frustration. They should not try to hide their emotions or stifle them but, when the moment has passed, they should think of positive ways to deal with this emotion. For instance, they might say, "I'm upset that Jonah said we would be watching a movie tonight then decided to stay home but maybe I can call Sarah up and she can come to the theater with me."

Let them know how to prepare for change.

If they will be attending a different school, going to a new friend's house, or meeting their best friend's family, let them anticipate a few changes they will need to make so that they meet fewer surprises along the way. By the same token, let them know that they cannot really identify every change they will need to make until they live through an experience and glean more information.

Reward your child for flexible behaviors.

On the days when your child plays with a new friend, reacts with resilience to a disappointing decision from a classmate, or agrees to try out a new activity with a friend, reward them in a way that is meaningful to them.

Dealing with Teasing

There is a difference between friendly teasing or "banter," and bullying. Teasing can be common in childhood for many reasons. Kids may need attention, they may tease to feel superior, or they may be mimicking what is happening in their own home (Freedman, 1999). If your child comes home one day telling you they have been teased, try not to overreact. Recall your own childhood—you probably encountered a bit of this behavior and may have occasionally teased your friends.

Encourage your children to be with kids who are supportive, let them know that a little banter is OK, and teach them to assert their limits if someone is going overboard. If they feel they have been insulted or bullied, they should let their teacher know immediately and also tell you about it when they get home.

Useful strategies to share with your child include:

- **Ignoring kids who are teasing** (because if your child reacts angrily, the teasing is only likely to increase in frequency and intensity). As mentioned above, if the teasing is constant or if it amounts to bullying, the teacher should be told.

- **Positive self-talk.** Your child should give themselves positive messages such as "I can take this. It will go away, it always does."

- **Agreeing with facts.** For instance, if another child tells your child, "You squirm a lot in your seat. You can't sit still," your child can answer calmly, "That is true. I find it hard to sit in one spot without moving."

- **Answering an insult maturely.** Your child might respond to a mean comment by saying, "Wow, that was an unkind put-down."

- **Using humor.** Laughter and humor can be some of the most powerful tools your child can count on in tough situations. It diffuses tension, shows the person insulting that they are missing their mark, and shows the kind of maturity and agreeable nature that make others want to be someone's friend.

To help your child make friends, ensure your home is a welcoming, safe, uncluttered space your child will feel happy to invite others to. Set up a few fun areas your children and their friends will love to play in—think a treehouse, slip-and-slide in the garden in the summertime, a vegetable garden others can tend to with your child, a volleyball net in your backyard, or basketball hoops in the driveway. If you have a free room at home, you can convert it into your child's playroom. Include toys, a sound system, and even a projector for your kids and their friends to feel like they have their very own "party space" in your home.

https://vivianfoster.com

HELPING YOUR CHILD STAY CALM AND POSITIVE AT SCHOOL

From the time your child starts school, it can be very helpful to see their teachers as your allies, advisors, and (when you're really lucky) your friends. Most children are at school for around six hours a day. During this time, they learn about the world, make friends, and form important bonds with others. Make sure you and your child's teachers are on the same page. Let them know how important they are to your child and how much you appreciate them. When they give you feedback, take it non-defensively and come up with useful strategies together.

Always let your child's teacher know that you are on their team. When you build a strong, positive, friendly relationship with your child's teacher, it becomes much easier to make requests that can enhance your child's learning experience. Discuss the following ways of making your child's school experience as positive as possible.

Adjusting the Classroom Environment

Your teacher can accommodate their classroom layout to make your child more comfortable. For instance, they can invite your child to sit in a place that is not too crowded or cluttered. If your child tends to daydream, then placing them by a window is not ideal. Seating them between people, meanwhile, can tempt them to chat. As mentioned by Paul Denton in his article, Seating Arrangements for Better Classroom Management (1992), flexibility is of primary importance when it comes to effective instruction. The subject being taught, the number of children in the class, and the natural structure of the room will all be determinative. Ashley Dewitz (2014) suggests the following accommodations:

- **Desk placement:** Kids with ADHD usually learn optimally when they are seated close to the teacher and/or when they are surrounded by attentive classmates. They work best in single seats, which are less distracting than those placed along with long tables with numerous classmates. Therapy balls can work better than traditional seats—for all kids, not just those with ADHD. Children should be kept away from visual as well as auditory distractions.

- **Visuals:** Rooms should not contain too many sources of visual stimuli, but teachers should use charts, tables, and images to attract attention to the material being taught.

- **Tidiness:** Kids prefer clean, tidy rooms since clutter can interrupt their ability to sustain focus.

Individualized Education Programs

Let your teacher know what works well for your child. Remember that they have many kids to teach and that their day can be full, busy, and sometimes, rather stressful. You can also consider sourcing an Individualized Education Program (IEP) or 504 for your child, which will entitle them to behavioral plans, extra time on tests, modified assignments, movement breaks, and more. To qualify for an IEP or 504, your child's school will first conduct an assessment of your child. Depending on your child's needs, the school may assign an IEP to them after meeting you first to discuss appropriate accommodations.

Learning Strategies

You can also discuss important points of focus during your child's learning process (Brock et al., 2010). These include:

Task duration: Your teacher can accommodate your child's needs by breaking up big tasks into smaller ones and by ensuring your child does not have to focus too long on one task. If possible, your child should enjoy small breaks so they can return to their work with a clearer mind and better focus.

Task difficulty: If assignments or tests are too difficult for your child, they may become unmotivated and give up. If your teacher sees fit, they can give your child easier or shorter tasks to keep them excited about learning and to boost their confidence. They can also give them a bit of extra time and attention to help your child hone the basics of a subject before jumping to more advanced subject matter. If a teacher is setting a task for the class that they suspect may exceed a child's attentional capacity, they can reduce the length of the assignment, valuing quality over quantity.

Direct instruction: Children with ADHD can benefit from teacher-directed rather than independent seatwork. They can benefit from learning how to take notes. Cognitive training or attention training sessions can also be helpful. In this type of training, attention is divided into attention orientation (directing a child's attention to a stimulus), selective attention (choosing one stimulus instead of another), sustained attention (keeping one's attention on one stimulus), and divided attention (dividing one's attention between two or more stimuli). Each of these skills is strengthened through teacher-directed activities.

Peer tutoring: Peer tutors with good behavioral skills and a good academic record make great tutors for children with ADHD. Brock et al. recommend that peer tutors be the same age and gender as the student with ADHD. Another type of peer tutoring that can work well is class-wide peer tutoring. In this model, all students play the role of tutor and tutee. The child with ADHD should be taught how to tutor others and be given supporting academic materials to enable them to shine. Tutors should receive immediate feedback and receive rewards for a job well done.

Scheduling: Children with ADHD tend to be more attentive in the morning, struggling with skills like problem-solving in the afternoon. Teachers should observe if this is the case and try to adapt learning to a child's schedule. They can also give children preferred tasks before non-preferred tasks to keep them motivated

Novelty: Kids with ADHD can be motivated with new material (i.e. material that varies in nature, texture, shape, and the like). Teachers can also use fun, colorful pictures, films, skits, and other means of learning that veer from standard textbook-centered activities.

Structure and organization: *We have spoken in other chapters about the importance of structure and routine. Children with ADHD don't like being caught off-guard. Teachers should use a consistent, day-to-day routine so kids know what to expect. In class, teachers can use aids like visual outlines that indicate which topics will be discussed on a given day. Structured lists help children when they have to study for tests and perform memory tasks.*

Rule reminders and visual cues: *Because children may forget behavioral rules in the classroom, visual rule reminders should be placed on classroom walls so teachers can easily point to one or more of them if required.*

Pacing of work: *Children should ideally pace themselves so they do not feel pressured to conform to a set speed or volume of work.*

Choice: *Kids with ADHD can benefit greatly from being given a choice regarding how they learn. Teachers can give them various tasks they can choose from and the child can choose the one that most appeals to them.*

Productive physical movement: *Children should be allowed to move. Teachers can either encourage children with ADHD to learn while walking or completing exercises or schedule frequent breaks involving physical activity.*

Active versus passive involvement: *Children can be asked to be actively involved in the lesson. For instance, the teacher might ask them to hold up visual aids or write important points on the board.*

Feedback: Brock et al. report that children with ADHD tend to respond better to cross-modal feedback. For instance, if they are completing a verbal task, they may respond better to visual feedback and vice-versa. A teacher might ask an oral question and give kids the chance to respond with a visual list.

Anticipation: Teachers should be aware of your child's needs and have the time to plan all the above-mentioned aspects. Giving them as much information as you can at the outset is important.

Enhancing Your Child's Learning Process at Home

Once your child is home, you are their tutor, mentor, and/or teacher. Take the above points into consideration, allowing your child to pace themselves and making sure they do not perceive disappointment, frustration, or irritation on your part. Talk to their teacher to discover useful strategies. For instance, if your child has three homework assignments, you might decide to start out with the subject they love the most so they don't feel bored from the get-go. Try to make work more exciting and easier for your child. Use learning tools such as mind maps, mnemonics, memorization cards, and the like to help them make sense of the structure of what they are learning and to help them retain information. Observe your child and try to create the ideal physical space and routine for them. Make sure you know what tasks they have to complete daily by asking for this information via e-mail or in the form of a communications book. If possible, ask the teacher for regular written feedback on your child's strengths and challenges.

Embracing a growth mindset

Let children know that their achievements and disappointments do not define them. Getting a D on a test today does not mean you cannot work hard to get an A next week. Growth mindsets are based on the idea that human beings are not static, fixed beings. Rather, we are capable of impressive, sometimes dramatic change but first, we must be honest with ourselves so we know what we want and need to change. Once this first step is taken, defining a strategy and measuring one's progress becomes considerably easier.

https://vivianfoster.com

16

LET ADHD WORK FOR YOUR CHILD

Seeing the positive sides of ADHD can enable you to fully enjoy every stage of your child's life with you, feel grateful for all they bring to your life, and build wonderful memories you can share with future generations. Studies have shown that gratitude is the key that unlocks happiness (George Mason University, 2009). By being grateful, you can be a role model for your child and help them both directly and indirectly. Researchers from Ritsumeikan University (Nawa & Yamagishi, 2021), for instance, found that keeping a daily gratitude journal for just two weeks can help keep students motivated.

Let me share a story of my friend Alana, who has been a mentor for me since the day I met her. Alana was my "parent trainer." As mentioned, from the time Neil was about six his team recommended behavioral training, which I took to like a duck to water—since I was keen to learn the myriad of ways in which I could make a difference to my son's life. Alana is an experienced professional and she also happens to be a mom of a daughter with ADHD. Alana's daughter, Nathalie, who is now 32, had many early learning challenges, and when Nathalie was growing up, finding teachers who were flexible and willing to make accommodations in the classroom was much harder.

As a child, Nathalie was what her mother called "obsessed with pets." She would shun schoolwork but spend hours reading up on dog and cat breeds, brushing her dog Shiloh's fur, and bathing him. Nathalie found it hard to concentrate in English and math but loved science and thrived under the guiding hand of a teacher who was touched by her passion for the health and well-being of animals. Her teacher was amazing and a shining example to educators as she always found ways to keep Nathalie interested, adapting homework so that Nathalie could incorporate her love for animals into essays, tests, and other tasks. The same child that seemed to find it hard to sit still or who used to daydream in French class used to sit so close to her science teacher that her friends used to tease her and ask her if she was the teacher's assistant. Today, Nathalie is a popular vet in our area. Her "hyperfocus" persists to this day and manifests itself in an insatiable appetite for reading about her specialty (Cardiology).

However, what really sets her apart from many other vets is one thing: She is always there for her patients. When other vets may refer emergencies to other clinics, Nathalie is "that vet" who gets up at 3 a.m. to attend to pets in distress and who sometimes stays up all night to monitor their progress. Whenever I think of Nathalie, I recall the words of airline mogul, David Neeleman, who once said, "If someone told me you could be normal or you could continue to have your ADD, I would take ADD." Neeleman believes that qualities like disorganization, difficulties in concentrating, and procrastination, are often accompanied by creativity and risk-taking—factors that are key to success in business and entrepreneurship.

Alana and Nathalie were the first persons to really open my eyes to the futility of fighting against who my son was. Instead, I saw my job as that of helping Neil make the most of the unique gifts he had and of giving him the tools (both material and psychological) he needed to be his happiest self. Through the eight-step method, I very much feel that Neil's is a story of overcoming obstacles with confidence. His is a success story.

Qualities Associated with ADHD

As mentioned previously, people with ADHD are often said to be creative and innovative. Despite the fact that a link between this disorder and creativity has not been firmly established, there is no doubt that there is a strong link between unusual and unexpected life experiences and innovation and creativity.

A child who shows inattention, for instance, can be prone to daydreaming, and this act in itself can provide children with a rich, complex, place to "escape" to. Fantasizing can also help one generate ideas, images, and thoughts for a creative writing or visual arts piece.

In research published in the Journal of Creative Behavior (White, 2018), researchers asked 26 university students to invent and draw fruit from an alien planet. The results showed that those with ADHD drew more unique fruit. Secondly, participants were asked to invent product labels. Once again, those with ADHD came up with more unique names. People with ADHD can be more impulsive and therefore more willing to try out new things without fear of failure. This can enable them to push their creative (and other) limits!

In one study published in the Journal of Psychopathology and Behavioral Assessment (Humphreys & Lee, 2011), a group of 203 children aged between five and ten were asked to undertake a Balloon Analogue Risk Task. The latter involves virtually "blowing up balloons" by clicking on the mouse. Children get points for inflating balloons but lose points when they overfill a balloon with air and it pops. The results showed that children with ADHD pumped the balloons up more than those who did not have ADHD. Their actions were indicative of their willingness to take risks to achieve their goal (in this case, to earn more points).

Of course, ADHD is not the same for everyone, and symptoms, behaviors, and interests vary from child to child. The above-mentioned studies are mainly interesting to me as a parent of a child with ADHD in so far as they show that children like Neil, Nathalie, and so many others can excel at activities, tasks, and professions that require their specific strengths. They are also a wake-up call to parents to start "thinking outside of the box" and stop trying to create "cookie-cutter" children. Allow your child to be different from the rest and help them realize that their difference is their superpower.

Jobs Kids with ADHD may enjoy when they are older

There definitely is no exclusive list of professions for people with ADHD, since each person has his or her own interests, abilities, and experiences. However, ADDitude mentions a few jobs that can gel with children's natural skills (ADDitude Editors, 2021). They match characteristics such as energy, enthusiasm, hyperfocus under pressure, and more, with professions such as teaching, daycare work with toddlers and preschoolers, journalism, copy editing, cooking, working in beauty and/or hairstyling, entrepreneurship, emergency first responding, nursing, technology, software development, artistic creation, and stage managing. The next time your child is feeling a bit despondent about their future, pull out this list and tell them a bit about the many people with ADHD that have achieved so much success that they wouldn't dream of a life without the disorder that may have posed seemingly insurmountable obstacles earlier in their lives.

For now, encourage your child in the direction of their authentic truth. Allow them to be different from the rest and let them know that their uniqueness is their superpower. Avoid labeling and putting them into a box of "what children with ADHD are supposed to be like." When they feel low, remind them of the words of Ralph Waldo Emerson: "To be yourself in a world that is constantly trying to make you something else is the greatest accomplishment."

PRIORITIZING SELF-CARE

Being a parent of a child with ADHD has its stressful moments. It is sometimes a bit of a "juggling act" because on a given day you may also have to speak with staff at your child's school, try to find ways to ensure your child has opportunities for social interaction, and (perhaps) need to take your child to therapy or attend therapy yourself.

Other obligations and relationships with their own set of needs and demands can include your relationship with your spouse or partner, other children, older family members, and friends. I remember feeling exhausted sometimes when Neil was younger and I still make it a point to check my stress levels and stop for a breather when I need to.

I found that during Neil's early years, I tried too hard to prove to myself and others that I could do it all— hold down my full-time job, take the kids to school, take Claire to after-school classes and Neil to therapy or appointments, keep the romance alive in my marriage, and still manage to meet friends every week or two. Although on the surface I was managing to keep it all together, I found that my character was changing. I had always been calm but I was starting to become irritable, feel some "road rage" while driving in traffic, and feel a little angry because I no longer made time to go to the gym. Sometimes I would have an anxiety flare-up, with a racing heart and breathlessness. These were all signs that I couldn't really give my best self to my loved ones if I was neglecting myself.

Self-care or self-compassion (being as kind to oneself as one is to others) is a vital and powerful buffer against stress. In fact, one PLOS ONE study (Ferrari, 2018) found that self-kindness can protect people against the harmful effects of perfectionism and help keep depression at bay. If you find that you are constantly trying to please others, you find it hard to say no, or you have so much on your plate that you aren't getting enough time to enjoy good sleep quality and quantity, it's time to start prioritizing yourself more.

The Importance of Exercise

The Department of Health and Human Services recommends that adults get at least 150 minutes of moderate activity or 75 minutes of vigorous aerobic activity (or a combination of both) per week.

Strength training a couple of times a week is also recommended. Exercise not only helps you stay in shape and keeps obesity, heart disease, and type 2 diabetes at bay, but it also staves off depression. A Karolinska Institutet study (Agudelo et al., 2014) found that exercise produces changes in skeletal muscles that filter away a substance that harms the brain and accumulates in the blood during stress.

Make sure your child is active too! Research from the Endocrine Society (Martikainen, 2013) showed that exercise could be a vital buffer against the effects of daily stressors such as public speaking.

Coping with the Inevitable

When a stressful event happens, you can employ various cognitive strategies to stop you from becoming anxious or from losing your cool. These include:

Keeping your ultimate goal in mind. *Your child may be taking longer than usual to get dressed and complete all the steps in their routine one morning but instead of getting so stressed that you end up rushing to school and work, think long-term. Doing so will enable you to accept that some days will be better than others and that, slowly but surely, your child will get better and better at sticking to their routine.*

Delaying your response. *Instead of being "reactive" (giving in to triggers and provocations), don't aim to solve all problems immediately. If you and your child are in a tense situation, consider talking about it after you have both had time to take a few deep breaths, and reflect on the situation. People find it much harder to listen to and understand each other, let alone to make a commitment to changing their behavior when they are defensive. Forcing the resolution of conflicts too quickly results in just that—defensiveness and stonewalling.*

Broadening your focus. When stress is high, take a step back and think of how much you and your child have achieved together as a team. This is just one hurdle but you have already successfully jumped over so many, sometimes in record time. Focus on all these positive achievements instead of the few stumbling blocks you meet along the way.

Practicing relaxation techniques. There are many tried-and-tested ways to relax but you should choose one or more that work the best for you. I remember when Neil was younger, a friend invited me to a yoga class. Yoga has been found in study after study to be a powerful means of lowering stress hormone (cortisol) levels. It is used in so many settings—from cancer recovery to PTSD and depression. However, yoga didn't work for me. My clumsiness and lack of balance made it hard to perform all the required asanas. So I tried something else—meditation. I went to a stupa, where free meditation sessions were offered and I felt a wonderful sense of calm afterward. Since then I have embraced meditation in many ways—I love the apps, Calm and Headspace and I also use audio files, which have timed sessions that include music and creative visualizations. I have tried many types of meditation—including mindfulness and transcendental meditation—and they have become my daily treat—one of the things I look forward to the most at the end of a long day.

Of course, there are a plethora of unique ways to relax and restore body, mind, and spirit that may resonate with you. These can include:

Getting away for a restorative weekend. Visiting a health resort or completing a yoga or meditation course is great when you are feeling overwhelmed. Often, these resorts include healthy, restorative foods that can energize you and help you to feel your best.

Embracing a healthy lifestyle. I mentioned the importance of following a Mediterranean diet and trying to avoid refined foods made with too much salt, sugar, or unhealthy fats. Keep alcohol consumption to recommended limits and avoid chemical substances as well.

Forming part of a sports group. Research by Harvard Divinity School researcher, Casper ter Kuile (Burton, 2018), indicates that in today's world, gyms specializing in activities like CrossFit are filling a spiritual gap felt by younger generations. He says, "People come (to CrossFit classes) because they want to lose weight or gain muscle strength, but they stay for the community. It's really the relationships that keep them coming back." Community-focused activities like CrossFit can help you release stress, gain greater insight into what you value in life, be an important source of support, and enable you to meet others who inspire and encourage you to achieve your goals.

Social interaction. Psychologists sometimes refer to happiness as having many "glasses" in your life filled— including the respective "glasses" that represent your professional life, family life, friendships, and more. Life can get very busy when you have children but don't limit your time out of the house to being a "soccer parent" or chauffeur for your child. Enrich your days by meeting friends, dining out, going for a walk on the beach or in the mountains, and more. Friends can add joy, understanding, and love to our lives in very unique ways.

Practicing shared parenting if you are separated or divorced. Maintaining a good relationship with your ex can be very difficult if the circumstances of the separation were not ideal. However, there comes a point at which you and your ex once again need to work as a team with respect to your child. Be open to the information and advice that each other brings, be flexible to your ex's suggestions, and keep each other informed on how different strategies at home and at school are progressing.

Identifying and altering negative thinking patterns.
Mindfulness meditation encourages people to recognize and accept negative emotions without suppressing them. Even if you do not meditate, try to be aware of the thinking cycles and patterns you use which are unproductive. Allow yourself to feel sad, angry, frustrated, and disappointed, knowing all the while that these emotions (like all others) are passing. They do not define how you feel about your child as a whole and they do not determine your child's future. Don't feel like you have to hide emotions from your children, either. Research suggests that there is a high emotional cost for parents who "put on a happy face" and overexpress positive emotions with their children. One study found that doing so leads parents to experience lower authenticity, relationship quality, emotional well-being, and even responsiveness to their children's needs (Le & Impett, 2016).

CONCLUSION

I once read that difficult roads often lead to beautiful destinations and of all the discoveries I have made in my lifetime, the one that touches me the deepest, surprises me the most, and makes me happiest, is being a parent. When you have kids you always assume things will go smoothly and easily. You aren't really prepared for health challenges that can test your patience, make you feel insecure about the choices you are making, or result in social and/or academic obstacles for your child.

When you have a child with ADHD and they have just received their diagnosis, you may be scared, shocked, and worried at first, but it is necessary to always keep your mind's eye on your goal and to stay positive despite the criticisms you may hear, your worries about whether or not to try a new therapy out, or the days when your child comes home and tells you something that every child will probably tell their parents at some point in their lives: "The kids at school didn't want to play with me today."

Start out with the understanding that no child is perfect. In the same way that work has easier and more challenging people and tasks, so, too, does school present your child with people with different levels of empathy, kindness, and good-heartedness. Your job as a parent is not to "make the ADHD go away," but rather, to give your child tools that can make their learning and social experiences as positive as possible.

I hope my book has helped you understand more about the nature of ADHD and the extent to which it is still a subject of much debate—especially in the medication versus behavioral therapy divide. As a parent, all you can do is research, speak to professionals and parents, and read up on ADHD. Ensure that any decision you take is based on trusted information and your thoughts and feelings about what is best for your child.

In earlier chapters I also went through concurrent conditions and the process of evaluation and diagnosis—something that is important to opt for earlier rather than later so you can start learning how to raise a child with ADHD. My eight-step program is behavior-based. It is the product of all my research, parental training, and experiences with Neil. I found that helping Neil "rewire his motor system" and encouraging him to play games to improve his motor skills boosted his confidence in powerful ways. I also discovered that reducing the sensory overload at home helped him stay calm and focused when he met other kids for playdates in the park or in our or other people's homes. As much as I made it a point to learn about ADHD, I also prioritized teaching Neil to be self-aware. One cannot really progress without knowing one's differences, weaknesses, strengths, and passions. Self-awareness is strongly linked to accountability: the idea that despite challenges, we still have duties to ourselves and others.

Some parts of my method are centered on learning and here, metacognition—or "thinking about thinking"—plays a key role. I used to love learning more about why Neil was so passionate about art, why he loved spending hours blending colors and finding the right hue for sunsets, and why drawing animated works was such a challenge. Knowing what you like and don't like can help you structure your learning, budget your time, and stay on track. Learning isn't always "fun" and it is normal to find some subjects more interesting than others. Some aspects of learning—such as honing one's working memory—can be challenging but they can be greatly improved through positive reinforcement and sensory games.

Three steps are specifically focused on home life. They include helping your child build their self-esteem through games and activities, creating a positive environment at home (by eradicating negative family patterns), and ensuring your child follows a sound nutritional regimen, gets good sleep, and exercises regularly. I also discuss external environments such as school and social situations, which are so much more within your scope than you may think. From the start, enlist the help of teachers and build a solid team that works together to create the most positive learning environment possible for your child. Help your child make friends by inviting them to take part in positive community groups that have a zero-tolerance for bullying and ostracization.

Finally, don't forget to work on yourself. You are your child's biggest hero and their most passionate advocate. You prepare their meals, give them a comfortable home, and get them to school and the myriad of appointments and extra-curricular activities that improve their quality of life. Don't forget to slot in a little "me time" into your schedule. Get the exercise you need to stay physically and mentally fit, pamper yourself with experiences that give you a lift, sustain friendships that make you feel supported, and remember that you are more than just a parent, spouse, or employee. You deserve to feel happy, fulfilled, and passionate about a few things that are all your own.

Thank you for reading my book!

I sincerely hope that it has helped you and that you and your child will benefit from implementing the strategies discussed.

I would be incredibly grateful if you could take a few seconds to leave me an **honest review or even a star rating on Amazon.** (A star rating will only take a couple of clicks).

Your review will also help other parents discover this book, and it might help them on their Parenting Journey. Also will be good Karma for you.

Scan to leave feedback or Stars:

https://vivianfoster.com

A FREE GIFT FOR MY READERS!

Included with your purchase of this book is your free copy of:

"Kids and Electronics 9 practical strategies to help you manage and limit your children's screen use"

Scan the QR code below to receive your free copy:

https://vivianfoster.com

If you loved *"A Beginner's Guide on Parenting Kids with ADHD"*, you might also love Vivian's other book:

"Anger Management for Parents:

The ultimate guide to understand your triggers, stop losing your temper, master your emotions, and raise confident children"

Grab your copy by scanning the code below:

https://vivianfoster.com

Made in the USA
Monee, IL
08 May 2023

33320508R00109